I'll Be OK, MA

Kirk House Publishers

I'll Be OK, MA

A Mother Receiving Signs from her Deceased Son

PHYLLIS SCHWARTZ

First Edition
Paperback ISBN 978-1-952976-55-1
eBook ISBN 978-1-952976-56-8
Hardcover ISBN 978-1-952976-57-5
Library of Congress Control Number: 2022907772

Cover Art by Rodisley Da Silva
Cover and interior design by Ann Aubitz

Published by Kirk House Publishers
1250 E 115th Street
Burnsville, MN 55337
Kirkhousepublishers.com
612-781-2815

TABLE OF CONTENTS

INTRODUCTION

I started writing this book after publishing my memoir in 2021. I wanted to tell the rest of the story about our son Danny, who died in 1985 at the age of 22. Dan was killed in an accident on his college campus just two days before he was to graduate. The main thing I want to convey is how he has been sending messages to us ever since.

We all have different experiences when a loved one passes. But mine might be unique. When I was 22 years old, and while feeding my eight-week-old baby, I had a clairvoyant visual experience that he was going to die when he was 22—I not only saw the date, I saw the scene. As Danny got older, he would give me signs and messages that he knew it too! But we could not stop the inevitable. As a massage therapist, I gave massages to many people that told me that they also had had a premonition that their loved one was going to die, but *none* of them knew the date or saw the scene. My mind was crying for help, but no one could help me.

I really didn't believe that this was going to happen. But when it did, I asked Dan to send me signs and messages that he was OK. That is what he always told me he would be—that he would be OK. And in my heart, I knew it, but I had to hear it again and again. And for 37 years, he has never wavered—I get signs and messages all the time. Even when I don't ask. Thanks, Dan.

To say the least, "the knowing" was horrifying. This book is not to give you answers on how this horrible event could've happened or why. Unfortunately, I don't know. I don't have any answers to this.

But for some reason that I cannot explain, I could not stop this tragic event from happening. Was it a force field or something like that that stopped me? If we all supposedly have our own path and our own life script, can another person change it? Evidently, a mom can't. Maybe our destiny cannot be changed—unless you change it yourself. I don't know. Why couldn't I just go to school and get him? I would give my life to have stopped this. I would take a bullet for my kids, chop off my head, and put myself in front of a firing squad—I wouldn't care. This whole thing does not make any sense. It's unbelievable, it's unfathomable, it's incomprehensible, yet it happened to me. I have thought about this a million times over. It is just unexplainable. I went into the deepest part of my heart for the answer—-but I found none. I asked my brain to explain it—but I had no answers. About a year before Danny died, he was in Austria going to school. He sent us this quote from an Austrian poet named Rainer Maria Rilke. Maybe I'm just reading something into this, but I think he was preparing us for what was to come. Here are the words:

Have patience with everything unresolved
in your heart and try to love the questions
themselves as if they were locked rooms
or books written in a very foreign language.
Don't search for answers, which could
not be given to you now., because you
would not be able to live them. And the
point is to live everything. Live the
questions now. Perhaps then, someday
far in the future, you will gradually,
without even noticing it, live your
way into the answer.
~**Rainer Maria Rilke**

My wish for anyone reading my book is that you too can receive messages from your loved ones just as I have by watching and listening for them with an open heart—and that the messages you receive will give you inner peace, knowing that your loved ones are close and that they are OK.

To understand my story, you need to know where I came from and my upbringing. So, I am starting at the very beginning and I wanted to leave enough room for the reader to make up their own mind about my experience as we all have our own opinions and belief systems and that is OK. But this is a story about what has happened to me. So, here goes.

Love, Phyllis

CHAPTER ONE

MY BACKGROUND

My Parents

I was born on February 5, 1940, in the small town of Slayton in southwestern Minnesota. The world I was born into was still recovering from the economic losses of the Great Depression. And there were tremendous sacrifices made by the entire country as we entered World War II in 1939. This was a tough time to raise a family, as they rationed many food items and gasoline through the end of the war in 1945.

I was incredibly fortunate to be born to two amazing, intelligent people. My mother, Viola, was five feet, two inches tall, with dark hair and beautiful hazel green eyes. She had such beautiful long eyelashes that they looked almost like they could be false. Mother was a registered nurse, an education level way beyond what most women had at that time, especially in a small town like Slayton. She said that she had always wanted to be a nurse from when she was a little girl. She went to the University of

Minnesota, and during her time there, she could not go home to visit or leave during school breaks because of the expense of travel. Since she always had to remain on campus, she continued taking classes and received degrees beyond the title of RN. After completing school, she took additional training at Moose Lake State Hospital, studying psychiatric disorders. When she finally returned to Slayton to practice nursing, she ended up helping on her parents' farm during the day, and she would work at the Slayton hospital at night.

My father, Walt, was six feet, two inches tall, with blond hair. He was very handsome and had the most vibrant personality. My dad was also from Slayton, where his parents, who were dairy farmers, raised him. He lived with his parents on the dairy farm ten miles south of Slayton, whereas my mom lived with her parents on a farm ten miles north of Slayton. They attended high school together in Slayton.

Dad was an entrepreneur and a visionary, and he owned the first of many businesses in town. These businesses included the first Coast to Coast Hardware Store, the first bowling alley, the first plumbing and heating company, and the first Culligan Soft Water business. He was even elected mayor in 1940 while he continued to cultivate growth in the community by bringing electric lights to the baseball park to promote the local baseball team.

Although my parents had gone to school together in Slayton, they didn't start dating until 1931. A couple of years after they had both graduated, my mother began nursing school. While my mother was away at school, my dad planned to visit her on one occasion. He caught a ride from someone in town up to St. Paul and hitchhiked to the

U of M campus. When he got there, he wasn't allowed to see her because she was on duty and her nursing supervisor wouldn't let Mom off duty. Luckily, one of my mom's friends said she would cover for her, and my mom was able to go down and meet with my dad, where they sat under an apple tree that was in full bloom. Unfortunately, they were only able to visit for fifteen minutes before Mother had to return to her duties and Dad had to hitchhike back to Slayton. Their visits were few and far between, but their love grew despite this, and they soon began planning for marriage.

My parents were married in 1938. It was a beautiful wedding—my mother had ventured into her parents' farm field, where she picked wildflowers for her bouquet to walk down the aisle with, giving a special touch to the nuptials. But a sad tone hung over the wedding because Mother's brother, Francis, was not there.

About a year before the wedding, my mother had gotten home to the farm, where she lived with her parents, after working an all-night shift at the hospital. Her mother was baking bread downstairs, and her sister, Clara, was gathering eggs in the chicken coop. My mother watched from her upstairs bedroom window as her dad and her nineteen-year-old brother, Francis, cut down some big trees in the outer part of the yard. Suddenly, one of the large trees they were cutting down twisted unexpectedly and fell on Francis. My mother saw the accident, and she rushed downstairs, shouting for my grandma, her sister, and a hired man to help pull the tree off Francis. Mother knew it was terrible. They carried him to the car, and my grandpa began driving as fast as he could to the hospital that my mother had just come from. There had been a storm the night before, and as they rounded a corner, they saw the road was blocked off by pieces of trees and fallen limbs. My grandma and grandpa started frantically pulling debris off the road so they could get through. As they were doing this, my mother was in the backseat with Francis, holding his head in her lap.

He looked up at her and said, "Waa Wee," a name he'd called her since he was little because he couldn't say, Viola. "Am I going to die?"

My mother exclaimed, "No."

"Pray for me, Waa Wee," said Francis before shutting his eyes and dying.

When my grandma and grandpa got back into the car, my mother had to tell them Francis had died. Francis was only nineteen years old. What a scene that must have been, as he was the family's pride and joy. He had finished high school the year before and took a year off to help his father on the farm before college. He had plans to become a doctor and return to Slayton to practice medicine and help his father on the farm. My grandpa planted a weeping willow tree at the scene of the accident. Every day for years and years, he would go out to the tree and cry.

This memory was with my mother on her wedding day. Interestingly, after my parents' wedding, they asked my grandparents and Aunt Clara to go with them on their honeymoon. They all toured the Black Hills and sixteen other states on the drive to California to see the Redwood Forest. They were gone for six weeks, which was so good for them.

Fertility Rocks

About a year or so into their marriage, after trying without success to have children, my parents heard about a couple in Canada that had just given birth to quintuplets that had all survived; the five were known as the "Dionne Quintuplets." No other set of quintuplets had all lived before that time, so this was quite the story back then! The Red Cross of Canada had signed a contract with the Dionne family, saying they would agree to pay for raising the children, as the family had four other children already and was very poor. The Red Cross ended up selling the children's rights to the country of Canada, and Canada turned the children into a tourist attraction. The children didn't even live with their parents but instead lived across the street in a special house, surrounded by barbed wire, where tourists could come and watch them play. It is said that Canada made $50 million a year on the kids by selling souvenirs, pictures, autographs, and other trinkets. One thing they *gave away* were rocks gathered from the area, which they called "fertility rocks." My parents were willing to try anything, so after hearing this, my father decided to drive up to Canada and pick up one of those fertility rocks. He brought home one of the rocks (which is still in our family to this day), and lo and behold, shortly after, my mother became pregnant!

Her pregnancy was long and difficult, but the baby's heartbeat was strong throughout. When it came time for the baby to be born, everybody was in the delivery room to support her! My aunt Clara, Aunt Gladys, my mother's cousin Mable (all registered nurses themselves), plus at least five other registered nurses and her primary, Dr. Pearson, were all there (Mother worked with Dr. Pearson at the Slayton hospital, besides seeing him as her primary doctor.). Everyone was there when my brother was born, strong and healthy—nobody could believe it! What a miracle! After my brother was born, they had all kind of forgotten about my mother, as they were all rejoicing and high-fiving about the miracle baby. My aunt Clara looked over at my mother then and tried to tell Dr. Pearson she noticed something about Mother's tummy and that she thought there might be another baby in there! He didn't believe her at first until my mother said she felt she needed to start pushing again. My mother pushed, and I was born, the second of two miracles! Mother had decided to name us after her favorite priest at the University of Minnesota, Father Phil, and so there we were, Phillip and Phyllis.

We were both full-term babies, and we each weighed five pounds. The doctors explained that evidently, our heartbeats were in sync, which was why it sounded like one heartbeat every time Mother was at her appointments. In those days, they did not have ultrasounds, so they couldn't check the baby in the womb to confirm there was only one.

Ed Born

About a year and a half after Phil and I were born, my mother was about to receive another miracle. She discovered she was pregnant with my brother Ed.

With the arrival of Ed, there would be five of us living in a one-bedroom apartment! Shortly after Ed was born, my father decided we needed more space. He found a little two-bedroom bungalow one block away from Main Street and purchased it. In our new home, all three of us children slept in one bedroom, and our parents slept in the other bedroom.

We were in our new home, and everything was finally coming along. My father's businesses and my mother's job at the hospital were going well.

Polio Outbreak
About this same time, there was a big outbreak of polio all over the United States, particularly in Chicago. A call went out to all RNs across the country to go to Chicago and help in the hospitals to care for all the patients that had contracted polio. My mother, being the tenacious warrior that she was, volunteered to go help. She arranged for different groups of people to help my father take care of us kids while she was gone. She might be gone for a whole month.

After her last night shift at the hospital, she came home, packed her bags, and all of us went uptown to wait for the Greyhound bus that was coming to pick up the volunteer nurses from Murray County. While waiting for the bus, my mother got a bad headache. She sat down on the curb, then she laid down on the sidewalk, and her legs became so weak that she couldn't move! Dr. Pearson came running over, along with the other nurses and friends, to attend to her. They suspected that she had contracted polio and called for an ambulance to pick her up. Without hesitation, the doctor had her transported by ambulance to Minneapolis to the Sister Kenny Institute for polio. She was there for an entire year! It was so scary to see my mom taken away like that. We all cried.

The polio virus has been around since 1789, and maybe even as early as the fourteenth century in Egypt. In

1910, a major epidemic began in Europe and spread to the United States. It was most prevalent in summer. Swimming pools were closed, all theaters were closed, people wore masks, and people stayed their distance from one another. It was remarkably like the public health measures that we experienced with the COVID-19 virus in 2020!

The polio epidemic peaked in the 1940s and '50s, when many people were left paralyzed and many died from the disease. Over half a million people worldwide were killed by polio every year during that time.

Sister Kenny was a nurse from Australia who started a polio institute in Minneapolis. She violated the accepted rules for treating the disease that usually called for using splints and plaster casts to immobilize the patient's legs, with patients sometimes having to wear them for years. Sister Kenny promoted wrapping the legs in warm, moist packs, and she focused on moving the muscles. There was no prevention available until 1957, when Jonas Salk came up with a vaccine to treat polio.

My mother was treated with moist, hot packs and walking exercises. My mother told my younger sister, Frances, when she was older, that Sister Kenny had told her, "Do you want to be an invalid, or do you want to walk and see your children?" My mother told Sister Kenny of course she wanted to walk!

My mother followed the treatment administered by Sister Kenny no matter how painful it was and was able to walk again! During the year she was at the institute, she became good friends with Sister Kenny and loved her very much.

When my mother finally came home to us, my grandmas, my aunts, all the nurse friends, neighbors, and I all took turns to put moist hot packs on my mother's legs. I would help carry the hot towels from the kitchen to the bedroom. When the hot packs cooled, my mother would get up and walk very painfully around the house. One day, after carrying hot towels to apply to my mother's legs, I said to my aunt Clara, "What are these things on my hands? They hurt!" She replied, "Those are blisters, darling!"

Fran Born

On October 1, 1947, our dad dressed Phil, Ed, and me up and said he was going to take us for a little outing! We didn't know where we were going, but we ended up at Slayton hospital. He told us not to be scared and that this was going to be a happy event. We didn't know what he meant. We went into the hospital, went upstairs, and then down a long hall. At the end of the hall, there was a room where we saw our mother lying in bed, and right next to her was a beautiful baby girl! What a surprise! My mother named her Frances after her brother. Now there were four of us kids.

Calendars

Next to the back porch, on my mom's kitchen wall, always hung a crooked, pale-yellow calendar. It forever had black and yellow lettering on it, and on the bottom of the calendar hung a little pouch. Toward the top of the calendar, "STATE BANK" in big letters presented itself boldly. Every year at Christmas, the local bank would give out the calendars to their customers for the new year. When mother got a new calendar, she hurriedly transferred every birthday she had written from last year's calendar to the new one. She included birthdays for family, friends, and neighbors, and she would also write "passed" on the date for anyone that had died. In the pouch below the calendar, she would store all the monthly receipts. She was meticulous about it and never missed putting a receipt in it.

I believe I was about six when one of our neighbors died. Mom was in the kitchen making a hot dish to bring over to their family, and we were talking about death and dying, life and time. I guess I didn't understand the concept of time, seasons, or years of life, but suddenly I had an epiphany. I looked up at the calendar hanging on the kitchen wall and thought to myself, *Oh I get it; a person only gets so many calendars, which is how it goes. I get it. Your life goes left and right, just like the calendar. The calendar, just like life, does not always hang straight.* I understood life at that moment—you only get so many calendars. This brought back memories of my uncle Francis, who only lived nineteen calendars before he was killed in a tragic accident.

Our Tragedy

When I was eleven years old, we all noticed that our father seemed so tired. He should have been tired—good Lord. He had four little kids, was building a new addition to the house, had just bought a new car, was serving as mayor of Slayton, still had an early morning paper route, ran the Coast to Coast store, brought the Culligan Soft Water business to town, owned his own bowling alley, had a plumbing and heating business, and was thinking of starting a chinchilla farm outside of Slayton to employ more local people. He would come home from work, lie down in his reclining chair before dinner, and fall asleep. My little sister, Frances, was a daddy's girl, and she would try to wake him up by playing with his face and kissing him on each cheek, but she could not rouse him. Then my dad would grab her, and she would scream, and they would play their game all over again. Finally, one night in November, he felt exhausted and not feeling well. I asked him if he wanted a foot massage, and he said, "No, thank you," then he butted out his Lucky Strike cigarette and said, "This is the last cigarette I am ever going to have." We had dinner, and later all of us kids went to bed. Around eleven or twelve o'clock, I heard a noise and some commotion. We were remodeling our house, and some construction material had just been installed that separated my bedroom from the dining room. It had tiny holes in it about the size of a quarter, so I peeked through one of the holes to see what was going on. I saw my father rolling around on the dining room floor in excruciating pain.

Suddenly, my mother came running into my bedroom and said to watch Frances because she was taking our father to the hospital. The following day, we woke up with Aunt Clara, Uncle Ray, and Mother in the bedroom. Mother said she had some bad news, and we mustn't cry. I think that must have been the mentality of the 1940s and 50s—don't cry.

Mother said Daddy got sick in the night, and God took him away to his home in heaven. I threw up—Phil just stood there stunned—Eddie threw himself hysterically on the bed and cried—Frances, being too little to understand what happened, just started asking many questions. It was too unreal to imagine. Our dad had suffered a fatal heart attack. He only had 41 calendars.

Soon after, my father's death had spread through Slayton. People came to the house in hoards and hoards, bringing platters of pasta salads, sandwiches, hot dishes, cookies, and flowers. Around me, I could see people talking, laughing, and crying, but I didn't want to talk to anyone, so I took Frances into a bedroom to play with her. It looked like a party, and it was all meant kindly. We had grown up attending funerals and hearing about people dying, so I understood the concept of death. Later, some men came and removed my parents' furniture from their bedroom, and some other men carried my father in a coffin and put him in the bedroom—that's what they did in those days. The sun was going down, and there were eerie shadows in the bedroom. There was still a smell of the cigarettes he had recently smoked mixed in with a scent of flowers and my father lying there very still and cold.

We all had to kneel by the casket and say the rosary. My mother had so much faith and found so much comfort in prayer. I didn't like it at all. After the rosary was said, I heard some men in the back of the room talking about how the Catholic Daughters would stay the night with the body and the Knights of Columbus would stay the rest of the night with the body. I thought, "He's not a body. He's our dad." I climbed up on the red velvet kneeling bench next to the coffin and looked down on him. *No, no. Last night he was our dad, and now he's just a body. No.* "Where are you, Dad? We need you—wake up, wake up!" Later, every time I went into that room, day or night, for years, I would get flashbacks of the shadows and smells. I did not like that room. The funeral was huge, and when it was all over, we went home to no Dad.

Frances thought she saw Dad coming home for lunch and yelled, "Mama, Mama, don't cry—here comes Daddy." Coincidentally, the man next door looked a lot like our dad. He was about six feet tall with the same build, and he was always wearing a white shirt and dress pants. He always came home at the same time for lunch as Dad had when the noon whistle blew. It was so sad. How do you explain our dad's death to a four-year-old?

Grandpa is in Charge

Several days after Dad's funeral, our mother went back to work full time at the Slayton hospital, and we kids were left all alone. We all worked hard, but we also fought hard without parents or supervision. Phil thought he was the boss, and I thought I was. It was kids raising kids. During our fights, one of us would pick up the phone and call Brady, the telephone operator in Slayton, and ask her to call Mom at the hospital. Brady would answer and say, "Are you kids fighting again? Your mother is busy." We would all yell and scream for our mother so that Brady would ring up the hospital, and the next thing we would hear was, "Hospital—Vi speaking." We would all fight for the phone, and finally, she would say, "I'll call your grandpa."

Grandma and Grandpa Galles had sold their farm and moved to Slayton, and they lived only a few blocks from us. We would all be yelling and crying for our mom when we could soon see Grandpa pulling up to the house in his 1949 blue Buick to see what was going on. He was a tiny man, about five feet, six inches, and he weighed 145 pounds. He was constantly dizzy, and we never knew why. He never drank, but he would come staggering up to the front door, walk in, sit down on the sofa, put his hands on his head, and start crying. I would think, "What a softy." But then I would think he was worn out and could take no more. He had been through the Dust Bowl, the Great Depression, and World Wars I and II; he watched two of his children die (two-year-old Adaline died from pneumonia, and he watched as his nineteen-year-old son, Francis, was killed by a falling tree on his farm); he watched our mom fight through polio and then the death of our father. He sat there looking just plain worn out.

We stopped fighting and hugged Grandpa and cried with him. Mom always thought Grandpa would come over and say something to us and act as a parent. I don't think she knew he would come over and sit down and cry with us and we would take care of him. Those were not the best of times.

The Milk Bar
On the brighter side, I got so lucky, as my best friend Carol's sister, Colleen, had a job at the local movie theater connected to a soda fountain bar with about twenty stools and served ice cream, banana splits, popcorn, and candy. It was called the Milk Bar, and it served moviegoers and the general public.

The theater owner needed help at the soda fountain bar, so Colleen recommended her sister, Carol, and me for the job. We were only thirteen and a half but were hired anyway, and he paid us in cash, so I had additional money to give to my mom. Many of us working there had a single parent at home, and I think he gave us all jobs that he knew we could use to help our families.

I absolutely and positively loved it—all the kids hung out there—I had a home. I would start work after school, stay until the theater closed at around 11:00 p.m., then do the final clean-up of the Milk Bar. My friend Patty sold tickets to the movies at the ticket office and would also count the money for the day's receipts after closing. We wouldn't finish our work until 11:30 p.m., and then we would run home through dark alleys, which was scary. The workload left little time for me to study and prepare for school the next day. Also, I missed out on parties after the athletic games and other fun things because I was working.

I was a cheerleader by then, and I would bring my cheerleading outfit to work. I would work until game time, change into my cheerleading outfit, go to the game, cheer on the team, return to work after the game, and work at the Milk Bar until it closed, then put on my poodle skirt and saddle shoes and go back to the school for the end of the sock hop.

It was there that I learned to love ice cream. We did not have ice cream at home, as my mother did not believe in dairy products because she said, "When you are through nursing as a baby, you don't need any more milk. You could get all the nutrients you need from other foods." So the owner of the Milk Bar told Carol and me we could eat all the ice cream we wanted, which we certainly did. I think he thought we would get sick of it and that would be the end of that.

We would eat ice cream the minute we got to work. We built beautiful banana splits, milkshakes, and sundaes to eat. We would eat until our shift was over and sometimes make ice cream cones at 11:00 p.m. to eat on our trip home. We loved ice cream. Today, ice cream is still one of Carol's and my favorite foods. I cannot get enough of it. The owner of the theater and Milk Bar in later years went bankrupt. We often wondered if Carol and I were at fault because we had eaten up all the profits. I will always be grateful to the theater owner for giving me my first official job and work family.

Sweet Sixteen, Going on Seventeen

I had found my voice at the Milk Bar—my self-esteem, pride, and identity. I was blossoming. It was my party. Laughter, gossip, ice cream, and popcorn. I owned the Milk Bar.

The years went by quickly, and I was sixteen or seventeen. All of us Frerk kids had settled into our routines. In those days during the 1950s, no one from our groups dated exclusively.

One of the boys in the groups that hung out at the Milk Bar was Jack Schwartz, who lived next door when we were young. Mom would push Phil and me in a buggy, and Jack's mother, Viv, would push him in a stroller, and they would go for walks together. His mother and mine were good friends. But unfortunately, we lost track of each other as Jack's family moved to the other end of Slayton when he was a young boy.

We were grown up now, and Jack was a handsome, intelligent, and athletic young man. He was the basketball team captain; he was a four-sport letter winner; he was the Slayton Jaycee Athlete of the Year in 1956, and he was the high school homecoming king. He never seemed to notice me, but then he unexpectantly asked me to his senior prom at the end of his senior year.

Over the years, prom has become such a big, expensive production with many expectations. But back then, it was so much fun to be with your friends and have a particular date. No one had the kind of money that goes into it today. In fact, after the dance, we all enjoyed meeting up at Gillette's Drive-In for a hamburger and fries before being dropped at home. Simple, yet fun, and lots of good memories.

It was extra special to go as Jack's date to his prom, as I was the chairperson for the decorations that year. Every prom had a theme, and we used my idea that year for "A Bridge to Beauty." You walked over a bridge to enter the dance floor, and it was decorated beautifully with flowers, miniature lights, and waterfalls. It was like a little bit of heaven for such a memorable night.

It was a magical summer. Jack worked for his dad downtown at the Grain Belt Beer distributing company warehouse, and every chance he got, he would run over to the Milk Bar to see me. Sometimes he would go to a late movie and walk me, Carol, and Patty home from work after closing up at the Milk Bar. That fall, he attended college at Luther in Decorah, Iowa. Since he didn't have a car, he would hitchhike home on weekends to see me. In my senior year, I asked him to my senior prom. It was love.

My Senior Year of High School

Suddenly I was a senior in high school. Yippee. Where did all of my calendars go? It seemed like my dad had just died. I ran so fast—days, nights, weeks, months, years. I was so anxious for high school to finally be over.

I had an outstanding senior year. I marched and twirled my baton at athletic events and parades. I was a cheerleader for the basketball and football games. I was voted to be homecoming queen, and my twin brother, Phil, was voted to be king. It was a great way to end our school years. I invited Jack to be my homecoming date, and again after the dance, we went to Gillette's Drive-In for burgers, malts, and fries. My senior year was almost over, and I was so happy.

But there was also a sad note. Our dear Grandpa Galles died of a heart attack on Easter Sunday, April 6, 1958. He only had 74 calendars.

As we got closer to graduation time, I was hell-bent on *not* going to college, which was what was expected of me. Mother wanted me to become a nun and Phil a priest. That was her dream. I wanted to be an airline stewardess. In 1958, a stewardess was what they now call an airline flight attendant. One morning at school, there was an announcement on the intercom from Joyce, the school secretary, that I was supposed to go down to the school superintendent's office. What did I do? Anyone called to his office was usually called because they were in trouble.

It was so scary, as I didn't know what I had done wrong. As I sat down in the outer office, waiting to see him, I asked Joyce if she knew why I had been called to the superintendent's office. She said she didn't understand why he wanted to see me, but my name had been on his schedule for a couple of days. The door opened, and the superintendent motioned for me to come in and sit down on a chair facing his desk. I imagined the worst. Maybe he would throw me out of school or something, or perhaps I was flunking out of school and didn't know it. I told my crazy mind to settle down, as I had done nothing wrong.

He just sat there, looking at me for the longest time. My mind was yelling, "Hurry up, hurry up. What is this all about?" Finally, he said, "Well, I will make this short, and there will be no discussion about this." He said, "I hear you want to be an airline stewardess?" Breathing a sigh of relief, I smiled and said, yes. He said, "Well, your family worked long and hard to get you out of the fields and being an airline stewardess is nothing but a glorified waitress. You are going to college. If you want to be a glorified waitress in the sky, you go to college first and get your degree, and then you can do that. In the meantime, I forbid you from becoming an airline stewardess." He waved a piece of paper in my face and said, "This is an application for enrollment at St. Cloud State College. I am filling it out and sending it in for you. You may go now." He then got up and opened the door for me to leave.

I was just a kid, but I knew that was no way to talk to someone. To this day, I don't know if Mom put him up to it or if it was his idea. I got up to leave and gave him the old stink eye as I left his office. I was thinking, "He is not my boss. I will do what I want." But in the fall, I was off to college at St. Cloud State.

My Freshman Year of College

I loved it at St. Cloud State College. I tried out to be a cheerleader for the basketball team—got it. I tried out as a baton twirler for the marching band—got it. I tried out for dancing parts in some of the school musicals—got it. I had three fabulous roommates, and we are still all friends today.

Early in my freshman year, I heard about an orphanage outside of St. Cloud, and I could empathize with the little ones because I knew what it felt like to be alone. So, I called the head of the orphanage to ask if I could bring some of us college kids out to play with her kids on Saturdays. She said she would love to have us come to play. So, I got five or six college kids, and we played with the orphans on Saturday mornings. I taught some of them to twirl a baton; the boys played catch with the boys, and the girls read to the little ones. I named our group "The Players." No one had ever done that at the orphanage before, and we continued to go there every Saturday the whole time I was at school. I don't know how long it lasted after I left college.

At that time, Jack transferred from Luther College to St. Cloud State College, as his scholarships had run out, and he could no longer afford the tuition. He took time off to earn funds to allow him to enroll at St. Cloud in the first quarter of 1959. He enrolled in education classes to pursue a teaching degree in math, physics, physical education, and sports coaching. We had met up with each other again.

On the Road

In the last quarter of my sophomore year, my aunt and uncle asked if I wanted to go on a three-month vacation with them. Mother was furious. That was the first time Ray and Clara had stepped over Mother's boundaries. She said, "Absolutely not. I'm worried you may never go back to school if you do that. So, you may not go on that trip." But I wanted to go. I knew in my heart that I probably would never get another chance in my whole life to go on a three-month vacation. I had never been on vacation except once when Mother took us on a short trip to the Black Hills.

I broke out in a rash called pityriasis rosea that looked like measles due to anxiety. I was trying to decide whether to go or not go. If I decided to go, I would be going against my mother's orders. I finally decided to go on vacation, and my rash went away. Wow, was my mother mad! I packed my ragtag suitcase and off we went. We started with the Black Hills, then went to Yellowstone, and worked our way down to Albuquerque, where we went to the hot air balloon festival. There were hundreds and hundreds of beautiful hot air balloons that would go up simultaneously. It was something to see. Then we went on to the New Mexico state rodeo contest with hundreds of people dressed in cowboy outfits.

Next, we went to Sedona, Arizona—what a beautiful place—parts of it looked like Northern Minnesota. Then on to Nogales, Mexico, where I experienced my first bullfight—it was awful.—I felt like crying.

Next, we went to the top of the Baja Peninsula and up the coast of California, where we visited my uncle's cousin, who owned the Pacific Ocean Park. We stayed with him, and he gave us tickets for all of the park rides. Then we were off to Las Vegas, where we stayed for a whole week, where we saw shows and gambled day and night. Then we went back to Los Angeles, where we toured Warner Brothers Studios.

Next, we drove up the coast of California to see San Luis Obispo, where Ray was stationed when he was in the army; then we toured the Redwood Forest. Finally, we went up to Canada to see the Canadian sites, east to Minnesota, and home to Slayton.

I was anxious to get home to see Jack and see if Mother was still angry with me. She wasn't mad, and I was so relieved.

I planned to work the summer at the Milk Bar and the Slayton Drug Store and then go back to college in the fall. I had more credits than I realized, as I had carried heavier class loads my freshman year and the start of my sophomore year. I was almost done with my sophomore year, with a few more classes to take to qualify for the beginning of my junior year.

Our Engagement and Wedded Bliss

When I got back from my extended vacation, I got the shock of my life. When I arrived home, Jack gave me a diamond engagement ring. He had worked all summer on a road construction crew in the daytime and at the Grain Belt Beer warehouse at night to save up the money for the ring.

Now my mother would go ballistic. She had three rules: First, you must have a college degree. Second, you could not get married until you were 28 years old, and third, your husband had to be a Catholic. I was about to break all three rules. Oh my God.

I went home and showed my mother the diamond engagement ring—I thought she would faint. She said we must get down on our knees and say the rosary—she was shaking. I said, "No, I'm not going to get down on my knees to say the rosary." Boy, was I in trouble. Then mother went to her bedroom and slammed the door. She must have called into work sick because she never came out of her bedroom for three days. I didn't know what to do. Then, on the third day, Jack came down to our house, knocked on Mom's bedroom door, and went in and said, "Vi, I love your daughter. I know we are young, but I will take good care of her and help her go back to school."

Then Jack went out to Ray and Clara's resort on Lake Shetek to tell them the same thing he had told Mom. This was in June. We had both planned to go back to school the following fall quarter. As the summer went on, Jack and I talked about marriage and decided we would like to get married and then go back to school. Well, that threw Mother for a loop.

I went out to Ray and Clara's cabin at the lake to talk to Aunt Clara about our plans. Clara said, "I love you, darling, and whatever you want to do is OK with Uncle Ray and me. Go home, look at the calendar, and find a day your mother has off from work. Then tell your mother you will get married, and that is the date."

So, I went home and looked at the calendar and found she had November 5 off. So, then, before I lost my courage, I went right into Mom's room and told her that Jack and I would get married before going back to college in the winter. So, we set a date for November 5, 1960.

If her hair wasn't already gray, it would have turned gray. She never said a word and went back to her bedroom and started saying the rosary. It was June, and we had set our wedding date for November 5. Then surprise. In September, I discovered I was pregnant—I never told a soul other than Jack. My mother ran the whole town, and the town folks knew she did not want me to get married, so everyone was afraid to give me a wedding shower.

I went forward with the wedding plans without the traditional bridal shower. The wedding license cost 10 dollars, and the priest cost 25 dollars. I borrowed a dress from a girlfriend, Twyla, and the drug store owner gave me artificial flowers to make bouquets. After the ceremony, the ladies aid society served rolls and coffee in the church's basement. Mother had a hot dish for family and friends at her house. The total cost of the wedding for Jack and me was thirty-five dollars. Because Jack was not Catholic, the wedding ceremony could not be conducted at the altar in the church but had to be performed in the front aisle of the church, without decorations. The most memorable moment in the ceremony was when the priest gave out one of the loudest and longest belches I had ever heard as he was reading us our vows. I was stunned.

I could not believe what I had just heard. There was dead silence in the whole church. I think everyone was waiting to see my reaction. I turned to look at Jack's mom, Viv, who was sitting in the first row behind us, and our eyes met. We both got grins on our faces, and we laughed aloud. Then the entire church audience started to laugh. So, it went from what could have been an awkward and embarrassing moment to a funny moment. I never found out how the priest felt, and he never apologized. But I knew then that it's not what happens to you in life. It's how you choose to see it.

First Comes Love, Then Comes Marriage, and Then Comes...

We went to Arizona on our honeymoon, and I knew all the places to go because I had just been there with Ray and Clara. We came back to Slayton and lived in my mother's basement, where she charged us to rent until we went back to school in December.

We rented a darling tiny furnished apartment about four blocks from school, and both continued our education during the winter and spring quarters.

On June 14, 1961, I went into labor. I had not been home to Slayton since the previous December. So, it must have been a hell of a shock when Jack called Mother and said, "Phyllis is going to have a baby, and she is in labor at the St. Cloud Hospital." Jack's mother, Viv, my mother, Vi, and my sister Frances jumped into a car and drove up to the St. Cloud Hospital.

I delivered the most darling, beautiful little girl you have ever seen there. She had perfect little eyebrows, perfect skin, and a full head of black hair. She was lovely and healthy. We named her Jackie.

What a shock her arrival must have been for everyone. After the third day in the hospital, we left to drive back to Slayton with Jackie, and we stayed for the rest of the summer with Jack's parents. It seemed everyone in town came over to the house to ooh and aah over Jackie—she was adorable, beautiful, and perfect. She melted everyone's heart—including my mother's.

CHAPTER TWO

OUR FAMILY

Three of Us at College

The summer was going by fast! Jack had worked double shifts at Grain Belt Beer distributing to earn money to go back to school, find an apartment, pay for tuition, and pay for food for us. It was wonderful staying with Jack's folks. Jack's mom, Viv, made it fun and was so much help. Jackie had colic, and Jack wasn't home because he was working so much. As a new mother, I greatly appreciated Viv's help and support!

Viv's home was just like my mother's. The coffee pot was always on, and lots of friends and neighbors stopped by. I just loved it there. My mom would drop by to visit, or we would pick up the baby and go visit Mom. Then it was time for Jack to go back to St. Cloud for school. Jack borrowed Viv's car and drove up to St. Cloud to find a place for us to live that we could afford and be within walking distance of the college, as we did not have a car.

In hindsight, I don't know why I didn't stay in Slayton with Jack's folks and let Jack go back to school and come home to visit us when he could. I guess we thought we had to stick together as a family. All Jack could find was a furnished basement apartment that we could rent by the month and that was within walking distance from the school. He came back to Slayton, and the next day, in Viv's borrowed car, we headed back to St. Cloud. He had to make another trip back to Slayton to return her car and get a ride back up to school.

I had no crib for Jackie, so my mother gave me the bassinet that she used for me when I was born. I did not know what I was expecting when we walked into the basement apartment for the first time, but it threw me for a loop! It was about fifteen by thirty feet with a cement floor, unpainted cinderblock walls, and all open from one end to the other. There was a rickety old bed at one end of the room, an old table halfway down the middle, a shower and toilet, and a fridge, sink, and stove at the other end of the room. The linens and dishes were furnished, which was good because we didn't have as much as a blanket! The next morning, Jack left for school. There I was, in shock. What a contrast from the nice house I had just come from to a smelly, old basement that didn't even have any windows. I sat down on the edge of the bed and cried and thought, *What have I done?*

I didn't know what to do. All I could think of was to pack up Jackie and get out of the basement. I went for a walk and had to carry Jackie as I had no buggy or stroller. As I was carrying Jackie and crying and walking down the sidewalk, I heard someone yell at me, "Are you OK?" I looked up, and there was a lady about thirty years old, holding a baby, and three little kids hanging onto her legs, crying for attention. She yelled at me again and said, "My name is Janice. Where do you live?" I wiped away my tears and wandered over to her and introduced myself. I told her that I lived a block away in Mrs. Johnson's basement apartment and that my husband was going to school at the college.

Again, she asked me if I was OK, and I told her, "Yes, I was just in shock about where I have to live." She asked me to come in for a glass of lemonade and talk about it and to come back the next day for lunch. I had to get out of that basement, so every day for the next month I would pack up Jackie and walk over to Janice's house for lunch while Jack was at class. One of the hardest things about living in the basement (besides everything) was hanging up washed diapers to dry. The basement had a washer but no dryer, and I had to hang the diapers outside on a line to dry. That was a problem. I couldn't take Jackie outside with me because I had no stroller or buggy or anything to put her in, and I could not put her on the cold ground.

I couldn't leave her alone in the basement, and I couldn't ask the landlady for help as she was away at work all day. I remembered an old movie I had seen of African women who hung their babies in a pouch in front of them. So, I took a sheet and attempted to tie it around me to make a pouch—I wasn't very skillful at it and failed many times until, aha! I finally figured it out! Now I could take Jackie outside with me in my makeshift pouch to hang clothes out to dry.

A Better Home

After a month of living in that musty, smelly basement, we finally got lucky. My twin brother, Phil, was transferring from college in Bemidji to St. Cloud, and he had found a house in the suburbs of St. Cloud to rent with my other brother, Ed, and two other guys from Slayton. He needed more money to be able to pay the rent, so he asked us if we would be interested in moving to live with them and share the rent. We jumped at the chance to get out of that basement! Jack got a ride to Slayton and borrowed a Grain Belt Beer truck from his dad and loaded it up with a rollaway bed and linens from Viv, a couch someone gave us, a table and chairs Phil had found, and a few other pieces of furniture, and he drove our load up to our rented house. My friend Janice, who I had met when I lived in the basement, gave me a crib for Jackie. We were all set—five guys, me, and Jackie.

The people in the neighborhood were shocked to see all of us pulling up into a nice neighborhood in an old beer truck, looking like the Beverly Hillbillies, and hauling in old, junky furniture. We were the first commune in St. Cloud! We looked like a bunch of hippies. The neighbors were scared. They did not know what to think of us! On top of everything, they heard Jackie calling every one of the guys "Dada!" As the neighbors watched us move in with horror, we were not there for more than an hour and some of the neighbor men came to the door to introduce themselves and start asking us questions about what we were doing there. We explained the situation and who we were and what we were doing there. They calmed down, but you could tell they did not like what they were seeing. I'm sure they were thinking we were going to be a bunch of college kids having keg parties and marijuana parties and that we would have people coming and going all hours of the night. Who knows what went through their minds!

After we moved in, Jack drove the beer truck back to Slayton and somehow got a ride back to our new home. Then the guys proceeded to partition off the basement into bedrooms, as it was all open, using corrugated paper and cardboard that Jack had gotten from his dad's warehouse. They taped it all together and made room dividers so we had an apartment downstairs.

The longer we lived there, the more the neighbors loved us. The guys helped shovel the neighbors' driveways in the winter, carried in groceries for the wives, and helped the neighbors with their projects. The little neighbor kids would come over, knock on our door, and ask me if my *kids* could come out and play. How cute is that?

Then in late spring, it started to rain. My brother Phil headed downstairs after dinner, as it was raining, and saw water halfway up the basement stairs. Cardboard was floating all over, sleeping bags were floating, and everything in the basement was floating. We notified the owner of the house of the water problem, and he came over and said he wanted to sell the house and we would have to move out!

Now to top it off—I was pregnant again! We had no car, and Jack had been riding a bicycle to school, which someone had just stolen. Jack somehow found an apartment two blocks from the school where the apartment owner let us have the first month rent-free. No car, no money, and a second baby on the way. I cried and said again, "WHAT HAVE I DONE?"

While going to school, Jack got a job painting the dormitories on campus to earn money; he qualified for some financial aid and got some athletic scholarship money, as he was a captain of the St. Cloud track team. Times were tough, to say the least. He sold pop bottles he would find for five cents to the local grocery store. We didn't have a toaster, so we ate day-old bread we could buy cheaply and made peanut butter sandwiches. Our meals were spaghetti, peanut butter sandwiches, and fish that Jack caught in the Mississippi River near the college.

We furnished our apartment with the rollaway bed Jack's mom had given us, the crib my new friend Janice had given us, and used a big box turned upside down with a sheet over it for a kitchen table. We had one chair and no living room furniture, but the living room was carpeted. Jackie played with an old drip coffee pot that she could take apart and put back together like a pro. She also had some Tupperware to play with that I would put rocks in that she could shake to make noise. My grandparents also had given us some wooden blocks and empty thread spools that she could play with. Our next-door neighbors gave me some old magazines that contained pictures of animals and colors that I would look at with Jackie to entertain her. By then Jackie was twelve months old, had twelve teeth, weighed nineteen pounds, and had a 20-word vocabulary, including putting two words together. So precious!
We did not have a car, so Jack borrowed an old Chevy Coupe from his dad so I could get back and forth to the doctor. It was the only time we drove it because we could not afford to buy gas, which was 25 cents a gallon. I didn't even have three cents to buy stamps to send a letter to my mother. That is what a stamp cost back then.

The Second Surprise
Danny was our second child. The pregnancy was easy, and the baby was due at the end of September, but the

baby did not come. When I thought that my tummy could not get any bigger, the doctor finally agreed to induce me two weeks after the due date. I remember vividly as we pulled up to the hospital for me to be induced that there was lightning, it was not raining, there were no thunderstorms or anything like that. There was just lightning and lighting and more lightning. That was so strange. It was like the Fourth of July with sparklers going off. I said to Jack, "I think the universe is celebrating that the baby is finally coming." Danny was finally born on October 11. He was huge and weighed ten pounds, and he was perfect. I left the hospital two days later and went back to Slayton.

Jack went back to school at St. Cloud and I stayed with Viv, as she was the one who had a crib for Danny. Around October 20, Jack came back to get us and we all went back to St. Cloud.

Jack's Big Break

When we got back to St. Cloud and settled in, Jack sat down with me and said that while I was in Slayton, he met with his counselor to see if he could finish college early, as he had to do something to find a job to provide for his growing family. He had two quarters left to obtain a teaching and coaching degree. They determined he had enough credits to change from a Bachelor of Science degree to a Bachelor of Arts degree in math and physics and graduate early in December. Thank God.

His adviser in the math department told him that the computer company Univac in the Twin Cities was hiring and looking for graduates with his math and physics education. So, Jack decided to be proactive and check it out. He called the personnel number at Univac that his math adviser gave him and set up an appointment for an interview. He got an appointment for the following week to meet with an interviewer at a Univac office in St. Paul. Unfortunately, he had never been to an interview, and he did not even have a résumé.

We were both excited but nervous because Jack heard they were only hiring one in ten applicants. He gathered up his grades and diploma-to-be and headed off to the interview, not knowing what to expect. The interviewer introduced himself as one of the managers of a computer department and proceeded to review Jack's grades (which were As) and the classes he had taken. He asked Jack how old he was, and Jack told him 23 years old. He asked Jack about his background, where he was from, and how he had gotten through college. Jack told him he worked his way through. The interviewer saw Jack's ring on his finger and asked if Jack was married. Jack said, "Yes, I am married and have two children."

He asked many more questions that seemed to go on for several hours. Finally, the interviewer left the room and was gone for about a half-hour. Jack didn't know what to think. Was the interview over, and was he supposed to leave? The interviewer finally returned to the room and said, "You've got the job." Jack was stunned—he almost fell off his chair. Jack asked him what the job was. The interviewer said it would be computer programming. Jack said, "I don't know anything about programming, and I have never even seen a computer."

The interviewer said, "If you are that smart and hardworking, we will teach you, and we want you to start work here in two weeks." Jack accepted the job. He was stunned and so excited that he didn't even ask how much he would be paid. Instead, Jack went into the lobby and sat down to go over what had just happened in his mind.

While he was sitting there, he noticed a local newspaper and, for some reason, opened it up, and there were ads for places to rent. In the first column, the first listing was a double bungalow on Cedar Avenue in Richfield, about fifteen minutes from work. He found a public payphone in the lobby, put in a dime, and called the number listed in the ad. The bungalow owner answered and said if Jack came right over, he would show him the place. What a stroke of luck.

Jack went right over and met the owner. It was a brand new two-bedroom bungalow. Jack explained our situation to the owner and said that he was just hired at Univac and looking for a place for us to live. The owner was impressed and said he would hold the place for us until we could move in. He said to let him know when we were coming and that we wouldn't have to pay any rent until we moved in. That was unbelievable. Nowadays, you would have to put money down to hold it and pay the first and last months' rent.

Jack drove to a gas station with an outdoor payphone, put in another dime, and called me. I was sitting on pins and needles, waiting for his call to tell me about the interview. Jackie was crying, Danny was crying, and I wasn't sure I had heard him right. I had to have him tell me the story three or four times. I kept thinking, "This can't be true." I was numb. I couldn't believe he had just accepted a job offer and found a place for us to live. Finally, we both had worked so hard to get this moment, so I broke down and started crying along with the two kids.

The next day after Jack had gotten home, we started to develop our plan about when and how we would move to the cities. After all we had been through, this did not seem like a big deal. It was a project we finally had control of and that felt so wonderful. It was like a miracle; everything was finally falling into place. All we had to move was a rollaway bed, a crib, and a bassinet. Luckily, one of the boys who had lived with us in the "commune" had a pickup truck and said he was going to the cities and would drop our stuff off at the bungalow for us.

We then headed for Slayton to see if we could charge some furniture at the furniture store. After we told the owner that Jack had just been hired at Univac, he agreed to let us buy some of the display furniture from the showroom floor at a discount. We bought a cheap Danish living room set that consisted of a sofa, two end tables, two lamps, and a rocking chair. We also purchased the showroom floor bedroom set consisting of a bed, mattress, headboard, and dresser with a mirror. The owner let us have the whole package for $250. In addition, Viv gave us a kitchen table and chairs, and we already had a rollaway bed for Jackie and a crib for Danny. We were all set.

Again, Jack borrowed a Grain Belt Beer truck from his dad, loaded up our new furniture, headed up to the cities, and set it all up. He came back to Slayton with the truck and loaded us all up in the borrowed Chevy Coupe, and we headed up to the cities to finally be able to live in a decent place. We were in hog heaven.

Jack started his job and found out he had to wear a suit to work, so we dug out his old wedding suit and white shirt, his dad gave him a couple of his old neckties, and off he went. Jack found out that one of the other new hires at

Univac lived close to us, so they carpooled together to save money. We had to return the borrowed car to Slayton, so Jack stopped off at the Slayton Auto, and they let him buy a cheap used car and make payments. We were waking up to our new reality. Jack's monthly gross pay was $500.55, and his take-home pay was $430.00. Our standard of living had gone up, but now we had all of these new expenses. Yup, we were living the American dream, and just like everyone else, we were in debt.

Premonition—A Heavy Secret

About two months after Danny was born, it was Christmas 1962, and we went home to Slayton for the holidays. It was a wonderful time with a house full of cousins, lots of babies, excellent food, lots of gifts, Christmas lights, and family love.

When we got back home from Slayton, we were all exhausted, so I tucked the kids into bed, unpacked a few things, and thought I would leave the rest for the morning. I fell into bed exhausted.

It was about six in the morning when Danny woke up to be fed, and Jackie was still asleep. It was dark and cold outside. Jack was getting ready for work, as he liked to go to work early. He was making a cup of coffee in the kitchen. As I walked by him, heading to the living room, he pointed to the window. It had snowed during the night, and it was just beautiful and looked like white frosting. I acknowledged how beautiful it was, headed to the living room, and snuggled into a soft, comfy rocking chair to feed Danny. Jack had plugged in the lights on the Christmas tree, and they looked so soft and pretty. The picture window in our living room faced the Minneapolis airport, and I could see the lights of the planes coming and going. Jack left for work. I looked down at Danny as I was feeding him and thought, *Where did he come from?* He looked just like my family, and yet, he didn't.

He was so beautiful, with blond, curly hair that looked like wings, a darling nose, and big hands. He was nursing so hard that I noticed tiny beads of sweat on his forehead. I found out later that babies don't sweat until they are about one year old, but he was sweating. I took off his blanket and unzipped his little sleeper. He was so hot, and then he seemed to cool down. I just kept staring at him and looking at him and thinking, *You are so darling.* It was warm and snug as we rocked in the chair with the Christmas tree lights glowing, and I thought, *What a beautiful baby.* I kept looking at him, and it seemed like I had seen him before, but I couldn't remember where. He was just an extraordinary baby, and I was blessed to have him. I was a tired mother and closed my eyes and let my mind go blank.

I could never have imagined that this beautiful morning would be the last time I would ever feel the same. Suddenly—WHAM—a white flash occurred on the side of my head, kind of by my right temple. It lasted less than a nanosecond. But in that second, I saw Danny lying dead on the ground with black pieces of metal around him and his right hand severely damaged. Trees were cut in half, and another boy was lying by him. I knew the date of the accident was May 22, 1985. It was something that I saw and that I *knew.* It was like a calm trance or something. My life had just been changed in a nanosecond. The vision I had just experienced would be a heavy secret that I would carry for more than sixty years. I felt like my whole life had just been stolen.

I put Danny back in his crib and called Jack. He had just gotten to work, and I told him something strange had just happened and that we were OK, but I asked if he could come right home. I think he could tell by my voice that there was something wrong. He said he would be right there, and when he got home, I told him what had just happened. I misinterpreted the scene. I told Jack that I thought there would be a war in 1985, and it was about the time Danny would be out of college. I learned later that I shouldn't interpret my premonitions and just say what I see. In that case, I saw the black metal, which I thought was an army tank. I later learned what had happened to me was called a "Clair Visual Experience." It's when you see something and know it to be true. I had this experience many times in the years to come. Jack just listened to me, and he didn't acknowledge that my vision happened or did not happen. He just listened. After I calmed down, Jack went back to work as he was new on the job.

After Jack left, I quickly got a phonebook and looked up insurance brokers. Finally, I found a broker and called the number, and a lady answered, probably a secretary, and I asked her how much it would cost to bury someone. She said about $2,000, so I told her I would like to take out some term insurance that would run out in 1986. She sent me the paperwork, and I signed up for Danny and paid for it in increments with my grocery budget. After that, it never crossed my mind that a funeral would cost a lot more 22 years later.

As the days went on, I slowly returned to being myself and tried to figure out what had happened to me that morning. I had never experienced anything like that before. Maybe I fell asleep and it was a dream, but I knew I wasn't sleeping in my heart of hearts; it wasn't a dream. I kept fighting with myself. I did not want to believe what had just happened, let alone what would happen to Danny. As the weeks went by, I tried to shake it off like the incident didn't happen to me, but the thought popped into my mind. I would try to push it back out. I would tell myself to forget it. I tried to pretend that the incident did not happen and again told myself to forget it, but I couldn't.

Later, as the years went by, it was always in the back of my mind. It was always there, and again I would try to push the thoughts away and put on my happy mask. I thought to myself, *Don't let anybody know this—they will think you're nuts.*

This was a profound experience—22 years of anticipatory grief.

Danny, our blue-eyed blond, at 1 ½ years
old with his sister Jackie.

Our Big Move Out East

After working at Univac in the Twin Cities for about two years, Jack was promoted from programmer to manager. The promotion meant we would have to move out to Pennsylvania since that was where the project was that he had been traveling to work on. He wouldn't have to travel anymore—yippee! That was great. Now the kids would have their dad at home.

Univac moved all of our belongings out to Pennsylvania, and we drove. I thought it was fun. We didn't put in long days on the road in the car, and the kids played and slept. We stopped to eat and stayed in motels (at least I thought it was fun). When we arrived in Philadelphia, we stayed in a motel while looking for a place to live. We had contacted a realtor to search for a house for us. About three days after we met with the realtor, she called and said something had just become available. It was a furnished home with a swimming pool and three bedrooms on an acre of land in Bucks County, north of Philadelphia. She said the couple who owned the home had gotten into a fight and split up. They took their personal belongings and toothbrushes, walked out the door, and put the house up for rent. We jumped in the car, looked at it, and took it on the spot. We figured we could store our belongings in the garage.

The area was so lovely. It was in Bucks County on Buck Road, right down the road from the Delaware River that divided Pennsylvania from New Jersey. It was a wonderful sightseeing area centrally located from everything like Atlantic City, the Pocono Mountains, New York City, Philadelphia, and the Amish communities. The neighbors were terrific when we moved in. They all came rushing to introduce themselves, and I couldn't get over their friendliness. I couldn't understand them very well because of their accents. If they called, I would hand the phone to Jack because it seemed like they were speaking a foreign language to me. But gradually, Jack said I was talking like them too.

One day, Jackie came home from playing with one of the little neighbor kids and announced that she wanted a cot. I asked her why she wanted a cot when she already had a nice bed. Finally, after about 20 minutes, we figured out what she wanted. She wanted a *cat*. She had picked up the local accent too.

Several weeks after we moved into our house, some neighbors that lived behind us who we had not yet met, as they had been on vacation, came over and introduced themselves. They looked to be about seventy years old. We were making small talk with them when Babe, the wife, looked down at Danny and said, "Oh, I see you have a cock-eyed kid." I was taken aback by her abruptness. Jack and I both knew there was a problem with Danny's eyes; we had noticed it when he was born. We had taken him to two pediatric ophthalmologists, who both said there was nothing wrong with his eyes, but we knew there was a problem. So when Babe said that, I said, "Do you think so?" She said, "Of course, there is a problem." I said, "Thank you. We think there is a problem with Danny's eyes too." Babe said she was going into her house to get a phone number for us of a famous eye institute in Philadelphia called the Wills Eye Institute. That was where they had taken their son to correct his eyes that were cockeyed. I did not like the term *cockeyed*, but I took the phone number from her and thanked her for her help.

The next day, I made an appointment for Danny to see the eye specialist. There was an opening, and we got him in right away. The doctors examined him and said he would probably need three or four operations to fix the problems with his eyes. They discovered that Danny had a problem with his eyes going up and down besides being cross-eyed. We scheduled the surgery, but no openings were available for several months.

Not too long after we moved into our house with the swimming pool—I did not even have all of our boxes unpacked—Jack came home from work and announced that the airplane his project was developing software for was being relocated to Minneapolis for installation of new Univac computers. He would have to travel back to Minneapolis to help with the installation. So, Jack would have to start traveling again. I couldn't even talk; my mind went blank. Now I was out in Pennsylvania, and I was alone again. I recalled my mother always said, "Bloom where you are planted," so I did.

I had pool parties, met all my neighbors, went for walks with the kids, and admired the beautiful local foliage. The installation of the computers was completed in a few weeks, and Jack was able to come back home to stay for a while. About this time, Jack's parents came out to see us; Mom, Fran, Ed, and his wife came out to see us too. While they were visiting, we all went to the World's Fair in New York City. We also all went to Atlantic City to see the boardwalk.

Once our company left, we took our family on weekends to see the area's different sites. We went to the Pocono Mountains; we saw the Amish country; we went to New York City again; we went to downtown Philadelphia and saw the Liberty Bell; we went up and down the roads along the Delaware River, visiting the many antique stores; we went to plays at the local theaters that performed the shows later featured on Broadway. We had so much fun sightseeing out there, and our home was fabulous because it was so centrally located. We could go someplace like Atlantic City in the morning and be home by night. The neighbors taught me how to make applesauce for the kids and make the local bread and rolls. We picked apples and berries. I loved it out there.

Jack started traveling again as the plane that his project was developed for was now located at Patuxent River in Maryland. He had to travel there to support the flight evaluations of the computer system. Jack was able to send some of the men that worked for him to support the project so that he could limit his travel and spend more time with us.

Then it was time for Danny's eye surgery. We had to bring him to a hospital in downtown Philadelphia right about dinner time the day before the surgery. That's what they used to do. You went to the hospital the night before the surgery. I planned to stay overnight. I just assumed I could. But much to my surprise, the hospital staff said I could not stay—no matter how much I argued. They kept saying that was the policy. I kept saying, "But he's just a baby,"—so they let us stay until he was asleep for the night.

The surgery was scheduled for eight o'clock the following day. We planned to get back to the hospital before he woke up so we would be there before they took him into surgery. We did just that. We arrived early the following day, and when we went to his room, he wasn't there. Where was he? His nurse said very casually, "He's in the children's ward." We both ran frantically to find the children's ward. We finally found it. It looked like an orphanage in Romania with twenty or thirty cribs, all with crying babies. My eyes searched for Danny. I spotted him standing and hanging onto the old white metal crib with bloody tears running down his cheeks at the end of the room.

I grabbed him out of that crib and held him tight as I ran out of the ward. I got into the hall and found a chair to sit down on. I looked at his eyes and saw that all of his eyelashes had been cut off. Suddenly, a nurse came running over to me as she probably thought I was trying to steal a baby. I told her I was his mother and asked, "What happened to my baby?" The nurse said they had some cancelations and took him to surgery early.

I was heartsick—my poor baby—we weren't even there for the surgery. Of course, we didn't get to talk to the doctor because he was in surgery. The nurse said the doctor had fixed the up and down problem and thought he could fix the crossed eyes, but we would have to wait and see. The nurse said the doctor would call us later in the day. We left the hospital and headed home. I must have held him tight for about a week and never let him go. He was just a baby. His eyelashes did grow back longer and more beautiful, and his eyes looked beautiful.

We lived in the house with a pool for a little over a year when our realtor called and said the owners decided to sell the house one day. So, we had to find another place to live. We moved into a new townhouse in the area that was close to a school that our kids could attend.

Danny at 2 years old

Our Return to Minnesota

It was about time for the kids to start school. Danny was three, and he could begin preschool, Jackie was four, and she could start kindergarten. In Pennsylvania, the kids were supposed to start school at those ages. So, the kids both went to school from 1:00 to 3:30 p.m. Luckily, the school was right across the street from the new home where we lived, so I could walk them both to school and pick them up. It was so perfect. We had just begun to settle in at the townhouse, where we had now lived for about four months when Jack came home from work one day and said he was being transferred back to Minnesota.

Univac was assigning him to lead a project of fifteen programmers back in St. Paul, Minnesota, to develop the next phase of the task he had initially been sent to

Philadelphia to work on, as the new computer systems being designed were located in St. Paul. So, off we went again. We decided that the kids and I would fly to Minnesota, and Jack would drive the car back. We made reservations at a hotel across the street from the Minneapolis airport called the Thunderbird Motel. The plan was that we would stay there until Jack arrived with the car and we could find a place to live. We boarded the plane to fly back, and each kid had their seat on the plane. Shortly after takeoff, Danny said he didn't feel well and wanted to sit on my lap. He was burning up. Jackie said she wanted to sit on my lap a few minutes later and didn't feel good either. I tried to get her on my lap and noticed that she was also burning up. Good Lord. I was alone on the plane with two sick little kids who had high fevers. I was so scared. I called the flight attendant for some aspirin, but she didn't have any onboard. She brought me some cold, moist clothes to sponge them with. Finally, the plane landed, and I don't know how I did it, but I carried the two kids, my purse, and my carry-on luggage to the baggage claim area.

I found a skycap to help me with everything and got a taxi to get to the motel. When we arrived at the motel, I asked the desk clerk if he could get me some baby aspirin and water and bring it to my room, which he kindly did. I sponged both the kids all night long to keep their fevers down. I had no idea how high their fevers were, but I knew they were high. The following day, they both woke up with chickenpox. I called the doctor, an excellent doctor we had before moving to Pennsylvania, and explained our situation. Believe it or not, she canceled all of her appointments for the day and came right over to the motel. I was crying by the time she got there but relieved that I would get some help. I was so scared for the kids because their temperatures were so high. She calmed me down, checked the kids, and gave them some medication for their fevers and anti-itch medication for their baths. She stayed with us for about two hours to monitor the kids' fevers before leaving. She came back the next day to check on us—what a godsend. I loved her.

The motel management found out there was chickenpox in the motel and that it was contagious, and they said I was being quarantined and could not leave our room. I couldn't even go to get ice, and the maids couldn't come in to change the sheets or clean the room. However, the motel workers could leave food and supplies outside our door on the floor, which worked out OK. After being isolated in our room for several days, Jack finally arrived and went right to the nearest grocery store and bought popsicles and things the kids liked. The motel manager gave us a little fridge with a freezer for our food. In the meantime, the doctor would call every day to check on the kids and even talk to them like she had all the time in the world. What a wonderful person she was and I thank her from the bottom of my heart.

Two days after Jack arrived, he had to go into the office to work, but he would look for a place for us to live over the noon hour. One of the men Jack worked with had found a place for his family to live in a new townhouse complex in Bloomington called Georgetown Park, and Jack went to look at it. The townhouse had three bedrooms, two baths, a nice playground, and it was close to schools and Jack's work. When Jack came back to the motel from work that night, he stayed with the kids, and I went to look at it. We decided to take it. By the time we moved out of the motel into the new place, we had been in the motel almost a month, and the kids were better except for scabs from the chickenpox. We were all getting a little stir-crazy. Our "traveling" furniture had arrived from Pennsylvania, and we were ready to move into our new townhouse.

We moved into our new townhouse, and it was so nice. Again, we were fortunate to have such friendly neighbors. We had only been in the townhouse for about a week, and the eye surgeon from Philadelphia called, asking about Danny's eyes. I couldn't believe the doctor was calling me. He said he was recommending an outstanding pediatric ophthalmology surgeon in Minnesota, and he had already called and spoken to him about Danny's situation. The nurse would be calling me to set up the corrective surgery.

Danny had the surgery, and this time it went well; we were there for it, and they didn't have to cut off his eyelashes. After the surgery, they sent Danny home with glasses. He was so cute wearing those little glasses, although they were always dirty and scratched.

Then came the Fourth of July, and my mom and Viv came to spend the holiday with us. We had such a wonderful time together. They left for Slayton on the fifth, and we all stood in the driveway and waved goodbye. Jackie and Danny settled down on the couch with popsicles to watch one of their favorite TV programs. Next, Jack and I went down to the basement to toss in a load of laundry. We hadn't been down in the basement for more than ten minutes when suddenly Danny came downstairs with some dirty napkins. I asked him where he got them, and he said he got them from the garbage. I told him to throw them away as they were dirty. I thought he must have brought them from the garbage container under the kitchen sink. Two minutes later, I had a funny feeling and ran up the stairs, and as I reached the top of the stairs, a neighbor came running in the front door carrying Danny, and Jackie was running right behind her. She said that the kids had climbed on the two-ton garbage container by the garage to throw some napkins away, and the container tipped over and crushed the kids. She said some men were nearby and came over and picked the big garbage can off of them. The lady laid Danny on the floor, and the front of his shorts was all bloody.

I pulled down his underpants, and blood squirted out of his penis about three feet. Oh my God. We laid him down in the back seat of the car and I sat with him, and Jackie rode in the front seat with Jack as we headed for the hospital. Before we left, I told the neighbor to call the Northwestern Hospital Emergency Room, explain what had happened, and tell them that we were on our way. When we got to the hospital, the doctors and nurses were outside waiting for us. They put Danny on a gurney and carried Jackie into the hospital. Danny was in shock and was bleeding out as they rushed him into an operating room.

They took Jackie into another room to examine her. She seemed OK except for a bruise on her hip and, of course, she was all shaken up. I just held her to keep her calm. More and more doctors kept running into the operating room, and then there came Dr. Grant, all scrubbed up for surgery. Finally, after two hours of surgery, a doctor came out and told us Danny was stable and that when the garbage can fell on him, he must have been sideways because it crushed his pelvis, which in turn tore his urethra off his bladder. The bladder was also torn, as well as his prostate. They had to stop the bleeding.

There happened to be a surgeon from the Mayo Clinic at the hospital when we brought Danny in, and the other doctors called on him to help with the surgery. The Mayo surgeon was the one who came out to talk to us and said he had never seen anything like this before, except on an older man who had been in a bad car accident, and he wasn't this severely damaged. So, Danny was taken into the ICU, and we all went in with him. Jackie was scared, so Jack took her home, and I stayed with Danny.

The accident happened so fast, and we had just had a great time with the grandmas. I kept replaying the scene in my mind, figuring out what happened. We had just gone down to the basement, and Danny was just sitting on the couch having a popsicle with Jackie and watching TV. I could never have dreamt that the kids would go out to the garage and climb up onto a two-ton garbage container. I started crying and couldn't stop. I was glad there weren't any nurses around to see me.

I thought, *Why did I go down to the basement?* I felt nothing but guilt. It was all my fault—the poor little things. Now I knew how my grandpa felt when the tree they cut down twisted and fell and killed his son. He felt guilt for the rest of his life even though it wasn't his fault.

As the days went by, Danny had a couple more surgeries, and he got out of the hospital on Thanksgiving Day. He had been in the hospital for over four months.

A couple of days after Danny got home from the hospital, our neighbor Lois came to see him. Lois had three boys about Jackie and Danny's age. She said she wanted to take Danny along with her boys to Theodore Wirth Park in Minneapolis to teach them how to ski. I told her no. His bones may have healed, but he still had a catheter, yet she was insistent. Finally, she said I had to quit babying him. She said she would strap the catheter bag to his jacket, and everything would be fine. Finally, he wanted to go so badly that I relented and let him go. Danny loved it, and that was the beginning of his lifelong love of skiing. Thank you, Lois.

About that time, Jack was busy on his projects at Univac and, by chance, had been contacted by a headhunter who was looking for programmers to work for Control Data in the Minneapolis area. Jack preferred programming over managing a group of people, so he interviewed for the job. He was accepted for a job that was for more money and less travel than he had at Univac.

Shortly after that, we decided to go on our first family vacation, just the four of us, and we drove to Texas to visit some friends. These were high school friends from Slayton, Margie and Larry Thompson, who had invited us down to Dallas to stay with them. We had so much fun as they had kids of the same age. The weather was scorching in Dallas, but they had a swimming pool, which was beautiful. Jack went fishing with Larry, and Margie took me around the area to look at model homes. I fell in love with the one-floor plan and asked the builder if I could have a copy of the blueprints. Much to my surprise, he gave me the blueprints. We continued our vacation and mostly hung out in the swimming pool. The kids loved it. Several years later, we were able to use a slightly modified version of the floor plan to build our dream home that, believe it or not, we are still living in fifty years later.

When we got back home from our vacation, it was time for Dan to have another procedure to remove the scar tissue that kept building up between his urethra tube and bladder. We called the hospital to schedule the procedure and were informed by the hospital that we could not come back for the procedure until we paid the balance of our outstanding bill that the insurance did not cover. We paid off the remaining bill with the money we had been saving for a down payment on a house. Danny had the surgery, and it turned out just fine. And we started over saving for our home again.

Well, surprise, surprise, I found out I was pregnant again. I had a great pregnancy. On March 2, 1969, I had a healthy, beautiful, nine-pound, two-ounce baby boy at two in the afternoon. We named him Chris. The nurses were so enamored with him that they carried him up and down the halls to show him off to everyone. I don't think you could do that nowadays. We had been saving for about two more years to build up money again for a down payment on a house. Our fund was growing ever so slowly when my uncle Ray heard about what had happened to us with having to pay the hospital and doctor bills. He offered to cosign a loan for us at the Currie Bank near Slayton for $10,000, which, with the money we had saved, would give us funds to begin looking for a house. So off we went, looking at houses and then deciding we would like to build a house using the house plans on our vacation in Dallas. Thank you, Uncle Ray.

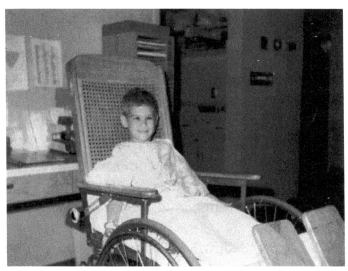

Danny recovering from a 2-ton garbage
container accident

Putting Down Roots

A flat lot to build a rambler-type house on was not easy
to find. We looked all over the west, southwest, and south
suburbs of the Twin Cities. Eventually, Jack found a lot in
Burnsville that was one-half acre. It was across the street
from a small lake and was available at a price we could afford. We purchased the lot and then looked for a builder
to build our dream home. We got a bid from a local builder
to make the home to the design drawings we had gotten
from our trip to Dallas. Again, the bid was within our price
range, so we contracted with the builder to complete the
home in the fall of 1971, so the kids could enroll in the local
schools. Our dream of a home for our family was finally
going to be accomplished. We had both worked so hard to
get here. The house was beautiful. It was about two thou-
sand square feet and had four bedrooms—one for each of

us—two fireplaces, a barbecue pit, a first-floor laundry room, and a full basement. We felt so blessed.

The kids were growing up fast; Jackie and Dan were only two blocks away from our house in elementary school. I would walk them to school every morning and pick them up in the afternoon. Jackie was in Brownie Scouts, which I was a leader for, and Dan was in Cub Scouts. Jackie was a beautiful little girl, and everywhere she went, people would stare at her and say how pretty she was. Dan was adorable, a good student, and such a big help around the house when Jack was always traveling with his job. Dan loved the Cub Scout experience. He won a pinewood derby contest by entering a race car he made all by himself. Other dads were building the cars for their sons to race, but Jack was too honest to cheat, and besides, Dan wanted to build it himself. We were very proud of him.

I watched Chris like a hawk as there was a lake across the street from us. He was only two years old, and I didn't want another accident. He followed the older kids around, and they loved him. They couldn't keep their hands off him, and when they came around him, he would yell and scream and run away. He didn't like to be hugged all that much. When they embraced him, they wouldn't let him go. Ha, ha. I don't blame him for wanting to run away from them. We were all very busy leading our new life in the suburbs, in our new house, and meeting new friends.

As we were becoming established as a family in Burnsville, Jack was still working for Control Data, commuting to the Plymouth office, and traveling to New York City to work on computerizing the Wall Street brokerage firms. Those were challenging times for us as a family—living in a new house, going to new schools, making new friends, and making it all work smoothly while Jack was traveling. All the kids chipped in, and we survived. On one of Jack's frequent trips to New York, he ran into one guy he had previously worked with at Univac. They discussed what each was doing. During their discussions, the Univac employee, now a director at Univac, asked Jack if he would be interested in returning to Univac to work for him for more money and less travel. Jack accepted his offer and started work for Univac two weeks later at an office in Eagan, Minnesota. Great. More money and less travel.

The minor travel part of the job did not last long. Soon Jack was promoted to a program manager position for military projects that required him to travel to Pennsylvania, California, Canada, New York, Washington, DC, Salt Lake City, Israel, and Singapore. One assignment required him to be gone 52 weeks and only home for one day on weekends. Thanks to the help from the kids, we managed to survive.

Our growing family: Chris, Danny, and Jackie

Danny, our pinewood derby winner

Buddies, Danny and Chris

The Tree

As Danny was getting older, I was getting more and more anxious about the date of May 22, 1985, as it was coming closer and closer. I had carried the premonition of Dan's death on this date secretly in my heart for years. Anybody who has had a premonition will know what I am talking about; those who haven't won't have a clue. Part of me said to myself that he would be fine, *Don't think about it, he will be fine.* The other part of me said, *This is real.* I was kind of out of my mind at that point; I was like two people, each fighting with the other.

I had a feeling that Dan sensed or at some level knew about his fate, but he never let on. I sure as heck did not know what to say to him about my premonition. Then one day something happened that confirmed my fears that Dan knew of his fate. One morning, Dan and I went to the 7-Eleven store in Apple Valley to pick up a few groceries, and as we were checking out, the clerk said, "Do you know this is Arbor Day, and we are giving away little trees, and you can pick one out as they are free."

I told the clerk, "Thank you, but no, thank you. We have enough trees in our yard." As I headed toward the door to leave, I suddenly felt Dan's hand on my elbow, and he said, "Mom, I want one." I quickly told him that we didn't have room in our yard, and there was no sun for one. He repeated it, "But Mom, I would like one." I saw his pleading face, so I said, "If you want one, pick one out. We will find a place to plant it."

He picked out the most beautiful little ash tree, and when we got home, we started laughing because we did not know where to plant it. We had about twenty huge trees in our yard and not much sunlight. We waited all day to watch for a sunny spot in the yard and finally found a place in the backyard with some sunlight. We dug a tiny hole, not realizing it was right below an electrical wire. We planted the tree, patted dirt around it, and watered it, and then Dan said to me as he gave the tree the last drop of water, "There—now every time you look at this tree you will remember me." I was stunned—was this just another coincidence? We both walked quietly back to the house, not saying a word, just holding hands. It was as if my heart weighed like a bag of cement. When you hear the expression "a heavy heart," I now know what that felt like and what that meant. Jack later had to move the tree from under the wires to a new location where it still stands today.

Danny after planting his tree

It's My Turn Now

One morning in 1976, I was reading the newspaper and noticed an ad for a massage school that was opening in Minneapolis. It was the first-ever massage school to open in the Twin Cities. I LOVED MASSAGE!

I thought back to a time when I had first learned about massage and how intensely interested I was at a very young age in what it could do for the body. I remembered when my mom returned home from the Sister Kenny Institute in the Cities, after having polio she got her strength back, had another baby, and went back to work at the Slayton hospital and she would take me along to work with her. I was about seven or eight at the time. She had Gramma Frerk make me a little white uniform, and I had white nylon stockings they found for me. It seemed OK with the hospital nurses that Mom would bring me along to work with her as they were all relatives of ours anyway. The doctors were also OK with me being there as a little girl to bring cheer to the patients.

I guess you would call me the first candy striper. I would pass out water, fluff the pillows, straighten bed sheets, deliver some of the food, and more. But what I liked best was when the nurses would show me how to massage.

When I saw the massage school notice in the paper, I thought someday I would like to be able to give massages. In order to do so, I thought I would have to have professional training and licensing and couldn't just say I was taught how to massage by my mother and some other registered nurses. With the support and encouragement from my family, I enrolled in the Minneapolis School of Massage.

I didn't have a massage table to practice on, so I put sleeping bags and blankets on top of the kitchen counter to use as a massage table. None of my family or friends trusted me to practice on them except Dan. Little did I know at the time that the classes I took from the Minneapolis School of Massage would help me to be licensed for my massage businesses and massage franchises.

As time went by in the '70s and '80s, the kids were getting older and were involved in many school and outside activities. Jackie was one of those involved in many activities both in and out of high school. She enrolled in a modeling class, called Barbizon, and had many fantastic experiences with that; she was elected snow queen in high school; she was the first runner-up in a Miss Minnesota contest; she was recruited by the basketball coaches for girls' basketball, but she had to drop out due to an injury. She was also an accomplished dancer and roller-skater, and she worked at a pizza place and a roller rink.

Dan was busy with varsity football; he was an avid weightlifter, and with a friend, they built a weight room in our basement. He was also an accomplished tennis player; he worked at a pizza place and helped a friend open up several Green Mill pizza shops. He could build anything and put anything together, and he was a great help to me around the house when Jack was traveling all the time.

Chris was very active in sports. He especially loved baseball and was on many traveling teams, which took up a lot of his time. He was active in many school activities, and he also was a big help to me when Jack was traveling. Time was passing rapidly—where did all of the calendars go?

By that time, Jackie was graduating from high school. She was a good student, but at the time, she couldn't decide whether she wanted to go to college. She decided to take a year off—which they now call a gap year—and worked in retail. She interviewed at a department store called Powers at the Burnsville Center and was hired on the spot! She soon was promoted to manager of a big department.

Dan was right behind her in school, going into his senior year and busy with sports, working, and chasing girls. Chris was on traveling sports teams, getting straight As in school, busy helping everyone, and in charge of everything!

Our family tree

The three amigos: Jackie, Chris, and Dan

Apprehension with Transitions

It was Dan's senior year, and my dark premonition was getting closer; obviously, I had never mentioned my premonition to Dan. Was it true? Was it going to happen? *Put your mask on, Phyllis,* I would tell myself and pretend everything was all right.

One night during the football season, I had a football party at our house for about twenty or thirty boys from the team. The windows and doors were wide open, and the beautiful fall evening breeze blew through the house. Everyone was having so much fun playing cards, watching TV, eating snacks, and roasting marshmallows in the fireplace.

I was in the kitchen making a huge pot of chili for the boys, and I don't know why, but I had all of the lights turned off in the kitchen except for the light above the stove. I stood there in the dark stirring the chili when I heard Dan's voice coming from the next room, and I started crying. I could not stop the tears, and an overwhelming feeling of extreme sadness swooped down on me. I couldn't stop thinking about Dan. I didn't want my tears to fall into the chili, so I grabbed the closest thing to me to block my tears, and it was a pink crocheted hot pad that Dan had given me. I couldn't see anything with the hot pad I had placed over my eyes, but suddenly, I felt an arm around me. It was Danny. He said, "I'll be OK, Ma." We both stood there crying and holding each other. I thought, *My God he knows—my God he knows.* I said, "Danny, I'm so sorry when you were little if I swatted you or yelled at you."

He said, "If you did, I deserved it."

I said, "No, you didn't, and I'm so sorry."

He said, "No regrets, Ma, no regrets. I'll be OK."

We both stood there holding each other and crying. Suddenly, one of the football boys came around the corner and said, "Hey, what's the matter? Did someone die or something?"

We never answered him. I just stirred my chili, and the boy went back to the party with Dan. I always felt Dan knew he would die young, but I never talked to him about it. I didn't know if I should or shouldn't speak to him. I didn't know what to do. But there seemed to be something like a force field that held me back from talking about it with him anyway. There had been many signs along the way that he knew, but I would brush it off, thinking that they were just coincidences. But now I knew that he knew too.

Should I see a therapist about this? Would they think I'm nuts? What do I do? Dan and I had a bond that sometimes seemed telepathic. I remember thinking, *I'd like to see a therapist buy into that one. They would think I'm crazy, so I'd better keep it to myself. I'll just keep my mask on.*

It was time for Dan to graduate from high school and to choose a college to attend. He was hell-bent on going to St. John's University. I didn't like St. John's. I didn't want him to go there. I hated everything about it, and I didn't know why. At least I didn't know why then. But after he had visited many schools, he said he still wanted to attend St. John's. He applied and was accepted, so Jack, Chris, and I drove him to school to move into a dormitory in the fall.

Halfway through fixing up Dan's room, Dan and I decided to go for a walk around the campus and left Jack and Chris to finish fixing up the room. We walked around the campus, and I didn't know where we were when big, dark clouds rolled in, and it got darker and darker. Then we came to this one spot, and we both stopped and stared at it. We both knew that this was where something terrible was going to happen. We hung on to each other and started to cry.

Thunder and pouring rain moved in, and we ran back to the dorm to help Jack and Chris put things away in Dan's room. I was still crying, so I went to an empty room across the hall to cry. Finally, it was time to leave, so we said our goodbyes and headed home. I cried all the way home. Chris was in the back seat, reassuring me that Dan would be OK. I knew this was not going to have a good ending. This should have been a happy time, but it wasn't for me.

Dan's high school graduation picture 1981

Building a Support System

As we were driving home from St. John's, I thought, *how would I position myself for this event if my premonition came to pass?* I would need support for myself and my family. Then I would think, *Don't go there.* Mom always told me, "What you think about, you go toward." My feelings were inescapable. I could no longer shut the thoughts out. The premonition kept haunting me. What if it turned out to be true? How would I explain this to someone? I sure as heck couldn't tell anyone about this. How would I stop it? The next morning after we returned home, I opened the morning paper and the "help wanted" ads jumped out at me. At the top line and first column was an ad for an assistant social worker for Dakota County.

I didn't have a social work degree, but I had two and a half years of college. Maybe that would work toward the job. It seemed like a sign. How much better would it be to be surrounded by therapists, psychiatrists, and psychologists if my premonition came to pass. The Dakota County Social Services office was only about a mile from my house. I didn't dress up. I just quickly jumped in the car and drove over to the office to pick up a job application to fill out. The receptionist asked why I was there, and I told her I wanted to apply for the job listed in the morning paper. She got up and went into another room, and all of a sudden, a lady came out and said, "I can see you now." I said, "Do you mean for an interview?" and she said, "Yes." I told her I hadn't filled out my job application, and she said that was OK. I could fill it out later. I told her I didn't want to waste her time and didn't have a social work degree. She said that was OK. I would work under a degreed worker (remember, this was 1981). Not more than five minutes later, she said I was hired, and I walked out with a job. I got back into the car and thought, *"Lordy, what just happened? What did I just do? Forty-five minutes ago, I was sitting on my couch, reading the morning paper, having a Coke, and now I have a job.?"*

I started the job the next week and was assigned to work under an experienced social worker. She was the most wonderful, intelligent, kind person to work with and a great teacher. We became excellent friends and even went on vacations together. Unfortunately, she died of a stroke a few years later (58 calendars). On my first day on the job, she told me to shadow her and meet the other workers in the group. Later that day, I met a worker standing by some file cabinets. I introduced myself and asked her what was in the cabinets, and she told me that there were files on various topics. If a worker needed help with something related to a client, the worker could make copies of the articles and give them to the client.

When the worker left, I opened the drawers and looked at the contents. There were topics on murder, abuse, incest, parenting, loss of self-esteem, depression, anxiety, and mental illness—every topic you could think of, but nothing on death, dying, and grief, which was what I needed. I heard of a therapist in Burnsville, a grief specialist who published many papers and books on death and dying. I thought that I would go over to his office to see if I could borrow some of his private files to make copies for Dakota County Social Services since the county didn't have any topics on this subject in their files. Sometimes I simply could not believe my stupidity, audacity, tenacity, or whatever drove me to follow up on my ideas.

I couldn't believe I walked into his office and asked the receptionist if I could borrow some of his private files to make copies. She looked at me like I was some crazy person that had just walked in off the street. She looked at me again, rolled her eyes, and reluctantly went into Dick's office. Pretty soon, he came out, and I introduced myself. I told him who I was and what I was looking for. I don't know if he saw the desperation in my eyes or the fear in my voice, but he said, "These files you want are originals and one of a kind." I didn't know what to say, so I just stood there, and then suddenly he said, "Mary, get a box and give my private files to Phyllis to make copies." I almost fell through the floor. I worked the next day to make copies of topics on death and dying and grief for the social service file and returned the originals to Dick's office by five o'clock that night. We all used those files for years, and I understand that they are still being used by Dakota County Social Services almost forty years later.

Now Dan was in college, Chris was doing well in school, and Jackie was thriving in her role as a department manager. The manager Jackie reported to lined her up on a blind date with her brother, Paul, who was just graduating from the University of Minnesota with a degree in engineering. They hit it off together and continued a relationship that eventually led to a wedding in Elbow Lake, Minnesota, in 1982. Jackie's husband, Paul, got a job with General Dynamics that required them to move to La Jolla, California. A year after their move to California, our wonderful first grandson, Ryan, was born, weighing ten pounds, eleven ounces. My mother, Vi, and I went out to California to be with Jackie one week before Ryan was due. Surprisingly, Ryan was two weeks overdue and required birth by C-section. Mom and I stayed another week to help the newest mother In our family, so we were there a whole month. They must have been sick of us by then, but we all just loved it with the new baby. I thought my kids were something, but when I saw Ryan, everything turned to Technicolor. He was so beautiful, happy, and healthy. What a gift to the world.

Dan's home from college for a family visit

A Trip to the Twilight Zone

Dan called us one night from college, all excited to tell us he had entered a contest at school and won a trip. It was a free, all-expenses-paid trip for two people to spend a week in Cancún. Cancún was opening to tourists, and it would be a fascinating trip for him. We were so happy for him. After we hung up, we talked about how hard it would be for Dan to pick a friend to go with him as he had so many. About a month later, Dan called and asked if we could take the trip tickets off his hands as he didn't want to hurt anybody's feelings by picking one person to go with him. We gladly accepted his offer as we had never been to any place like that before. So, a couple of weeks later, we went on a trip.

We were scheduled to leave from the Hubert Humphrey airport terminal. When we got there, it was very crowded and chaotic. While we were waiting to board the plane, we noticed three women hanging out together. One looked like a grandma, a college-aged girl, and one like the girl's mother. We commented to each other how cute they were. Then, over the intercom, the call came to board the plane. We were the first to board, and as we settled into our seats, the three women we had seen earlier walked by us, smiled, and took their seats farther back on the plane. We didn't see them again until we were taking a bus from the airport to the hotel, and we saw them get on the bus going to the same hotel we were staying at.

We had a great time swimming, relaxing, eating, touring, and shopping. One day we decided to take a bus tour of the Mayan ruins at Chichén Itzá. It was a scorching day with a temperature of 117°F. We started walking around with a tour group, seeing the fascinating sights, but I started not feeling well, so I stopped to rest. Jack went ahead and started climbing to the top of the pyramid, which at that time was open to the public. As I was waiting for him below the pyramid, I felt like I was going to faint, and there was no one there to help me. So I decided to make my way back to the bus. The bus had air conditioning, and our driver said he would sit in the bus and wait and keep the bus running to stay cool.

As I approached the bus lot, I was almost blacking out, and things were getting blurry. Then I got scared as there must have been fifty Greyhound buses, and they all looked alike. I didn't know where my bus was.

I thought to myself, *Get on the closest one*, which I tried to do, but it was locked, and there was no driver inside. So I tried the second one, and it was locked with no driver inside. I started crying and frantically tried to get on any bus. I thought I was having a stroke, and I'm sure my blood pressure was sky-high. I tried one bus, then another, and then another, and finally, a miracle of miracles, I came to a bus, and the door opened. I looked up, and there was our driver. He saw me, and he knew I was in trouble. He pulled me into the bus, where it was cool, packed me in ice, and gave me something to drink. As I was coming around, I glanced out the window, and there was Jack with his hand up to the glass, looking for me. What a scary experience.

The next day I didn't feel well and had a bad headache, so we thought we would just stay in our room and rest. Later in the day, I was feeling better, so we decided to go down to the open-roof lobby at the hotel that had tables and umbrellas and get something to eat. We ordered some food and drinks, and we started looking around and noticed the old lady we had seen earlier taking the bus from the airport, the one we called "Grandma," sitting all by herself. We decided to ask her if she wanted to join us, and she gladly accepted. She was so nice, and she told us she was in Cancún with her daughter, a teacher in Wisconsin, and her granddaughter, who was a student in college. She said that they always took vacations together. They had all planned to go to Chichén Itzá that day, but they had heard it would be hot there, so she decided to stay back and not go. We told her what had happened to me the previous day. We talked for about a half-hour, and then my headache started to come back, so we said goodbye and went back to our room. We spoke to each other about what we thought of the three ladies. How sweet that they all traveled together.

We didn't see the ladies again until two days later when it was time to leave for home. We were at the Cancún airport, packed with people coming and going. The airport was not finished as many of the side walls were still open, the roof was open, and the only place to sit was on low little beach chairs, and there were hundreds of people. We stood with our carry-on luggage and waited for someone to leave so that we could get a seat. Suddenly, Jack spotted two people getting up, so we quickly ran over and got the seats first. The chairs were spaced close to each other, and our knees almost touched the person sitting facing us. As I settled in my little chair, I looked up, and the person in the chair facing me was the grandma. We said hello, and I asked her where her daughter and granddaughter were. She told us they were checking the luggage, and she seemed pretty nervous about something and kept looking around. Suddenly, she stopped and said, "When I lived in Wisconsin, I was famous for palm reading, and my daughter did not like me to do the readings, but I did it anyway. I want to read your palms if you would like."

Jack immediately said, "No, thank you," but I stuck out my hand with enthusiasm and said, "Yes, thank you." Then she grabbed my hand, she said, "Number one—you will work hard pretty much for the rest of your life with your hands. Number two—you have a long lifeline, but you will have a couple of big bumps in the road on the way. Number three—you have three men in your life, and you will lose one of them."

Number one, I didn't know about working with my hands. I didn't know what that meant. I thought maybe gardening, but I didn't like gardening, and I wasn't thinking of massage at the time. Number two, I figured I would live into my eighties as that is what my mother and grandmother lived to be. Number three, I had three men in my life, and I would lose one of them. The three men in my life would be Jack, Dan, and Chris. I knew exactly what she meant—she was talking about me losing Dan. Just at that moment, the announcement came that our plane was ready to board. We quickly got up, and I looked for her daughter and granddaughter and did not see them. The grandmother said to me, "Phyllis, I'll be OK."

We had to board the plane and were seated way in the back, so if the grandma and the girls got on, we didn't see them. Maybe they were sitting in the front of the plane. It was absolute chaos when we got off the plane at the Hubert Humphrey airport in Minneapolis. People were all over, loudspeakers were blaring, and there were many customs lines. Jack and I got separated going through customs. He got in one aisle, and I had to get into another. We could see each other about five aisles apart, and when I looked to see how many people were ahead of me, right in front of me were the daughter and granddaughter the grandma had said were on vacation with her in Cancún.

I was so excited to meet them that I quickly introduced myself and told them how we had met Grandma and spent some time visiting her at our hotel and the airport in Cancún. I was babbling like a magpie when I noticed their faces. They were both staring at me, and I thought I was being too pushy. Then abruptly, the granddaughter turned to her mother and said in a booming voice, "I told you she was with us."

Her mother looked at me and said, "My mom died five years ago."

"NO," I said, "She just read my palm at the Cancún airport."

The mom said, "Yes, she was famous for reading palms, and I didn't like her doing that." I said, "Yes, I know, that is what she told us—what do you mean she died five years ago?"

The mom said that the three of them always vacationed together, and after the grandma died, they always knew she was still vacationing with them. I couldn't wrap my mind around what I was hearing. I said, "But, she had just read my palm."

The mom said, "My mom never missed a chance to get to know someone and read their palms."

The mom smiled, and then it was their turn to go through customs. They went through customs and headed to the front of the airport. I turned to look at Jack, and he was mouthing to me from a distant aisle, "Where is Grandma?" At that time, the front of the airport was all glass, and all of the taxis and cars would line up in front; I saw the mom and granddaughter get into a cab and drive away. I bulged my eyes and stared at Jack as if to say I couldn't believe what I had just heard. I felt like I was in the twilight zone.

The Year 1985

I was so excited that Dan was coming home from college for the weekend. I planned to take Dan and Chris out to Lincoln Del for lunch, one of our favorite restaurants, and everything on the menu was delicious. I was also very excited about our time together as I had a big surprise for

Dan. After we got seated, we chatted and placed our order. Then, we enjoyed our milkshakes and waited for our lunch to come when I announced that Dad and I had a graduation present for him. It was a 1985 gray Fiero.

He looked stunned, and he said, "You shouldn't do that, Mom. That's too much money. I will be OK; I will just use your Pinto for a while. I don't mean to be ungrateful." I started arguing with him and told him how proud we were of him and how hard he had worked to get through college. He was pushing back when I noticed the look on his face. He was staring straight ahead with a faraway look, looking right through me. Chris was jumping up and down in his seat, saying, "If you don't want it, then I will take it—I will have my license by then—I'll take it." Finally, I said, "OK, I've got an idea. We will get the car, and we will all use it." Dan looked relieved, and Chris looked ecstatic. Was I reading into this scene? I can still see Dan's face with that faraway look in his eyes. We got the car, and we all used it, except Dan.

It was Christmas, and Dan went to New York City with some of his buddies to watch the New Year's Eve ball drop. The new year would be 1985. For 22 years, every day and every night, every month and every year, I had dreaded that date, 1985, and here it was. We had a lovely Christmas, and Dan left a couple of days later to go to New York.

On New Year's Eve, we watched TV to see if we could see him, but of course, we couldn't with thousands of people in the crowd. He had told us where he would try to stand, but we never saw him. Finally, he returned home on the third of January, and Chris and I went to the airport to pick him up. In the paper, I had seen a big sale on ski jackets at Burlington Coat Factory in Apple Valley, and I knew

Dan needed a ski jacket for the following year. I knew Dan would be tired, and Chris didn't want to stop, but it was the last day of the sale, and the store was right on our way home. So I stopped anyway.

The store was packed full of jackets—hundreds and hundreds of jackets. The aisles were placed very close, with room for only one person to walk through. The aisles looked like tiny tunnels. It was eight o'clock, and the store was closing at nine. I started looking at the jackets fast, like running a race. Dan followed me. I said, "How about this one, Dan?" Then I would quickly pick out another one and ask, "How about this one? How about this one? How about this one? How about that one?" No comment from Dan.

It was not like I was worried about the time. Instead, I was saying, "How about this one for next year? How about this one for next year? How about this one for next year? Next year, next year?" I was getting frantic. I was going faster and faster. "Please say yes to a jacket; please say yes. Please, please, please."

Suddenly Dan grabbed me from behind and said, "Stop, Ma, stop." Then he said slowly and softly, "I won't need a ski jacket next year." I almost collapsed, and I hung onto him and started sobbing. He held me up so I wouldn't fall, tears running down his cheeks too. Then he said like I had heard him say before, "I'll be OK, Ma—let's go home."

Chris showed up at the end of the aisle and said, "Oh, there you guys are. I was looking for you. Why are guys crying? What's going on?"

Dan said, "Come on, Chris, we're going home."

Chris said, "Hey, I thought we came to look for a ski jacket?"

Dan said, "Well, Mom and I decided I don't need one."

A Tender Goodbye

Before Dan went back to school, he said he had a couple of presents for me. There were two of them. They were all wrapped up in nice paper with bows. How sweet. I opened the first one, and it was a darling little keychain with a little pig hanging on it. That was so thoughtful, as he knew I collected pigs. I opened the second one, and as I was opening the package, he said, "I know how much you like Willie Nelson." It was a tape of Willie Nelson playing and singing "Blue Eyes Crying in the Rain." He said, "Play it after I leave and listen to the words, Mom." So I played the tape, and I heard, "When we meet up yonder, we'll stroll hand in hand again." I shut it off. I couldn't take it. What was I going to do?

I called St. John's again to talk to some priest and told him about my vision and worries. I'm sure he thought I was a crazy mom. He just consoled me and said to be brave, pray, and everything would be OK, everything would be fine. I did not like his advice.

It was getting closer to spring, and I went out to get the mail one day and received a graduation card from my friend Margie for her son, who was graduating from high school in Plano, Texas. I opened the card, and the graduation motto jumped out at me in giant letters; it said, "ALIVE IN '85." No. No. No. Another sign or a coincidence?

Then something strange started happening. I had a little red Pinto station wagon; it was nothing fancy, but it had good mileage. I would always listen to some country western music while I was driving. Every time I would get into the car and start to drive and turn the radio on, it would be playing the rosary. The first time it happened, I thought that was strange, as that was not the station I had been listening to when I turned the radio off. So I turned the radio back to the station that I always listened to, and it happened again and again; the rosary came on, and it did it again and again and again. I thought maybe someone was playing a trick on me, but I always locked my car doors when I got out. It went on and on. I thought I was going crazy.

Time was running out, and this couldn't be true. What was happening to me? I was getting too many signs—this just couldn't be happening. Then one afternoon, I heard a car pull up into the driveway, and it was Dan. His buddy had to run an errand a couple of blocks away from our house, and Dan had hitched a ride. His buddy dropped Dan off at our house and said he would be back in about fifteen minutes to pick him up and head back to St. John's. Coincidently, I happened to be making some chocolate chip cookies, Dan's favorite. Just as he came in the door, I was taking the last batch out of the oven. I tried to talk Dan into taking my Pinto back to St. John's and was begging him, "Please take my Pinto. You will have things to pack up to bring home; please take my car." I pleaded and pleaded, but he said he wouldn't take it. Then we heard his buddy pull up in the driveway, and as he was ready to leave, we hugged.

That was to be my last hug from him. I thought to myself, *Notice where we are standing in the kitchen for this last hug, two feet away from the sliding glass door and two feet away from the kitchen counter. Notice the spot.* I laid my head against his chest. *Yes, this is how tall he is. This is where my head comes. Smell him. So sweet. That was Dan. Look at those darling, beautiful eyes, gorgeous nose, big hands, big feet, and wavy hair.* I held him tight and told him I loved him. Then as he was by the back door, he turned to me and said "Don't Worry Ma, I'll be OK." He jumped into the car with his buddy, and they took off. He didn't see me, but I chased the car up the hill beside our house until I couldn't see their car anymore.

I then fell into the empty field behind our house, crying hysterically. I knew that this would be the last time I would ever see him again. I don't know how long I lay there. I finally struggled to my feet and walked back home. I sat on the couch and stared into space. Jack was on a business trip, Chris was on a basketball trip, Jackie was at her home, and I was alone. I threw the last batch of chocolate chip cookies in the garbage. Dan forgot to take the second package of cookies with him. Finally, I thought to myself, "I've got to get out of the house."

It was getting dark, and a spring rainstorm was starting. I thought I would drive to the PDQ convenience store and get myself a Coke. I had to get out of the house. I jumped in the car and started backing out of the driveway, and there it came again on the radio—The rosary—No. No. No. I started pounding the steering wheel and tried to turn the radio off, but it wouldn't turn off.

We have a corner lot, so I drove to the street beside our house and parked the car beside our four pine trees. I jumped out of the car in the pouring rain, with thunder and lightning all around me, and started pounding on the car's hood. I was drenched, crying, and screaming like a wild animal. I don't know how long I yelled and screamed and screamed and cried. I laid my head on the hood of the car. I was numb and just lay there, but then I thought,

Maybe Mary was trying to tell me that she knew her son would die too. Talk about delusions of grandeur.

I just lay there with my head on the car's hood, with rain pouring down on me and thunder and lightning. I finally got back into the car, and I looked like I had been thrown into a lake. My hair hung, my mascara ran, and my eyes and nose were red and swollen, but the rosary had finally stopped. OK. OK. I said, "Whoever you are, I can't fight it anymore. You win. I give up. I have lived with this for twenty-two years, and my spirit is broken and gone." I abandoned my trip to the store, and I drove back to the house with a heavy heart. I collapsed into bed and cried myself to sleep.

Phyllis, the mom, the one side of me, was still fighting and saying NO. NO. I know whoever is reading this book will think I'm crazy. But when I was working for the county, some of my abuse victims told me they would split themselves at that time, which must have been what I was doing. So, I intuitively put Phyllis the mom in a little room she couldn't get out of. It was a small room, about nine by twelve feet, with a small white bed in the middle, no windows, a table, a little chair, and a little dim light in the corner. It seemed strange that the bed was in the middle of the room and not against the wall. So Phyllis the mom yelled and screamed and tried to get out, but she couldn't get out because the door was locked. She was hysterical.

I checked on her for years after Dan's accident, and she was lying down on the bed, quiet, and curled up in a fetal position. One day, several years later, I was checking on her, and she was gone. I don't know where she went— maybe we reconnected again, but she wasn't there anymore.

Strange as it may seem, about ten years later, while I was giving a massage, I looked up, and I was standing in the same room I had put Phyllis the mom in years before. The only difference was that the little white bed I had put in the middle of the room was not a bed but a massage table with white sheets. I couldn't believe it. There was a little table and chair in the corner of the room, with a dim light at the end of the room, and no windows and one door. Oh my God. This room that I had created in my mind was one of healing touch in which I had nurtured Phyllis the mom who had been in such excruciating pain from the thought of losing her son.

The next day after Dan had left for school, I called St. John's again, and they were of no help. I thought, *Help. Help. Someone, please help me. Just go get him and make him come back home.* And then I said to myself, *yeah, right before graduation, that would be cool for a mother to go get her kid and take him home from school.* Then something stopped me, like a force field that wouldn't let me interfere. Maybe people have their own life plans. I don't know. Something would just not let me go.

The time was going by. It was Mother's Day, May 12, and the phone rang. I answered it, and Dan said, "Hi, Ma." He sounded happy, and we talked about him finishing school and when graduation was. He then cried, said, "I love you," and hung up. Just then, Jack came into the house from mowing the lawn to get a drink of water. I told him Dan had just called, and Jack said he would like to talk to him. We called Dan right back, but there was no answer as Dan had made the last phone call before their house phone was shut off for the end of the school year.

Our last hug

CHAPTER THREE

DAN'S GONE

Dan's Accident

The day I had dreaded was finally here—May 22, 1985. Finally, finally, I got up and dressed to go to work. Dakota County social workers were on strike, and only a few of us were left on duty to handle emergencies. Jack showered and got dressed to go to work, and we didn't say anything to each other. We didn't know what to do.

I had an emergency to attend to in South St. Paul. A single mother and her three kids were evicted and had no place to go. So, I had to pick them up, and I didn't know where I would take them, but when I got to South St. Paul, I figured I had better put some gas in my car before I picked them up.

I put my hand on the gas pump, and WHAM. It was like a shock went through me. I stood there like I was being electrocuted. I knew it was Dan, and something was happening to him at that moment. Just then, another worker from the county pulled up to get gas, and I ran over to her and told her I had a family emergency and asked if she could take care of the mother with the three kids. She said, "Of course."

I drove home as fast as I could. I ran into the kitchen and sat down on the stool by the counter by the phone, and I just sat there. Then Jack ran in the back door and came over and stood beside me. Suddenly, the phone rang, a priest from St. John's. He said, "Is this Mrs. Schwartz?"

I said, "Yes."

He said, "Are you alone?"

I said, "No, my husband is right here with me."

He said, "Dan had a motorcycle accident right on campus."

I said, "I know."

He said, "I'm sorry, has someone already called you?"

I said, "No, Is he still alive?"

He said, "Yes, but hurry."

When we got to the hospital, I stood up tall and took a big breath as I entered the room where Danny was lying. Such intense feelings went through me that there were no words to explain how I felt. I had practiced for this moment for 22 years just in case the accident did happen. Also, remember I wasn't the real mother. Danny's mother wasn't there. The real Phyllis would've died right along with Danny. That's why I put her in that little room where she couldn't get out. She could pound and scream and do whatever she wanted, but she couldn't get out as the door was locked. I calmly walked up to the left side of the hospital bed. I put my arms around him—I did not want him to feel alone or scared. He looked just beautiful, just like he was taking a nap. A big white bandage was wrapped around his head, otherwise there was not a scratch on him. His skin was all tan from the spring sun.

I didn't notice who was in the room, but people kept coming. Dan's girlfriend, college kids, our family, and the college priests were all there, but it was just Dan and me. I put my hand on the side of his face and my mouth next to his cheek and ear. I had prepared for this moment for a long time, and I knew exactly what I would whisper in his ear. "Danny, this is Ma," I told him how much we all loved him and how proud we had always been of him. I told him what a wonderful son he had always been. *The things that I had told him so many times before.* Then I told him what had happened to him. That he had been going to the senior class picnic and lost control of his motorcycle and hit a tree. I told him that the doctor had said to us that upon hitting the tree, he had moved his brain stem two inches and that he would be paralyzed and would not be mentally right. Also, they were having trouble stopping the internal bleeding. I told him that we would take care of him forever and ever if he chose to live that way, and that was his decision to make. I put my hand on the top of his hand and said if you understand and hear what I have just said, move one of your fingers. Maybe it was just my imagination, but I positively felt his finger move. How could he do that if he was paralyzed? Perhaps it was just my wishful thinking. Then I whispered, "Danny, I don't know if it's true, but go toward the light if you see a bright light and decide not to stay here. You have always told me that you'd be okay so if you decide to leave, please send me a message that you're OK. I don't know where you will be, but I have to know that you're OK. Please let me know." Then again, I told him how much we loved him and kissed him good-bye. A strange thought entered my mind at that moment. When he was born, I got to say hello to him, and now I was saying goodbye. I kissed him again and again, then we all said the Lord's Prayer and everyone went over to his bedside and lovingly talked to him. My sister-in-law rubbed his feet, and everyone hung on to him. Then his incredible darling body died, and I'm sure headed toward the bright light in heaven—and his soul spread its wings and flew away with him toward heaven.

Our wonderful Danny died that night in the same hospital he was born in 22 years before and at the exact time he was born. My premonition had come to pass.

The Wake

The wake was packed with mourners. I stood there all by myself by the coffin. I looked down at our beautiful sweet 22-year-old son, who had just been killed on his motorcycle on his college campus two days before he was to graduate. Danny! I mentally yelled. Why did you do this? Why couldn't we stop this? How could this have happened? None of us can go on without you. Danny looked so beautiful. He had been tanning and looked healthy—getting ready for some job interviews. We had dressed him in his favorite outfit of jeans and a flannel shirt. He had hit his head on a tree, and consequently, he had white bandages on his head, so we put his favorite baseball cap on him. He looked just like he was taking a nap. He was so beautiful inside and out. I kept thinking to myself, *This just can't be true. This could not have happened.* But I knew it was true. *I know your body is here, but where are you?* I kept remembering when I was eleven, and our daddy died from a sudden heart attack, and I climbed up on the red velvet kneeling bench next to his coffin and asked him the same question: "Where are you, daddy? I know your body is here, but where are you. Wake up, Daddy, wake up." Daddy never answered, and he didn't wake up. So, then none of us four little kids would have a daddy, and now none of us would have a Danny.

For years, Danny had told me that he would be OK in different ways. We both knew that he was talking about the afterlife. He always told me, "I will be OK, Ma." If this horrible unthinkable accident has happened to Danny and Danny has left us, where is he? Where is he? I just had to know that he was OK. So I started pleading with him, "Please, please send me a message or a sign that you are OK. Please do not make it look like a coincidence. I will not notice it. It has to knock my socks off. Please send me a sign."

The pain was too deep for words. My grief was only comforted by trusting that he was OK. I don't know how long I stood there quietly sobbing and talking to Dan. Then, someone came up behind me, put their arms around me, and held me tight. After a while, I looked to see who was holding me. And just as I turned, I heard someone whisper clearly and softly in my left ear, "Don't worry, Ma, I'm OK." Good Lord. Nobody knew those words except Dan and me.

To my surprise and astonishment, there was no one there. I was still standing all alone. Dan was there with me—-invisible but there. Was I making this up in my mind? I don't think so. I was his mom. He was holding me and whispering to me that he was OK. This was his first message to me.

We buried Danny in the Slayton Catholic Cemetery next to my mom and dad.

To this day, I stand in the exact same spot in the kitchen where I gave Dan his last hug. I pretend I'm hugging him, and I put my head on his chest and smell his smell just like before when I gave him his last Great Big Hug.

We had borrowed an angel.

Dan, our borrowed angel

CHAPTER FOUR

STORIES ABOUT DAN

*These are some sweet stories about Dan
that our family holds dear*

Carving

Dan was a very precocious little boy and so sweet. When he was about four years old, we would ask him what he wanted to be when he grew up. (I think just like most parents do, just kidding with them.) He would always say, "I want to be a carver." We never understood what he meant. What did a little four-year-old know about carving? So, one day, when he was going crazy about wanting to carve, I gave him a big bar of Ivory soap, a popsicle stick, and a toothpick. He seemed so relieved. He sat down on the living room floor, and I put a towel under him to catch his soap shavings. Within minutes he had a darling miniature horse carved with all the details. I couldn't believe my eyes. It had perfect eyes and tail, and ears. From that day on, whenever he would get bored, I'd give him a new bar of Ivory soap, a new popsicle stick, and a new toothpick. He would whittle away. He carved animals, flowers, trees, and rabbits. I lined them up on the kitchen windowsill—then I'd line up more carvings on the living room windowsill—then the dining room windowsill. He would get quite upset if I tried to take them down, so I left them there. When people would come over for a visit, they would ask, "Who did those carvings?" They were always astonished when I told them Danny did. How could a little four-year-old boy carve things that were so precise and perfect? What did he know about carving in the first place?

The Library Trip

When Danny was four, I would take him and his sister, Jackie, to the town library. Danny would look around and around in the children's section, but he did not like the books in that area. I kept finding him in the adult section of books. I asked him what he was looking for and if I could help him find it. But he said he did not know what he was looking for. Week after week at the library, he would browse in the adult section of books and not want to go to the children's area to find a book. Then one day at the library, he came running around the corner where Jackie and I were looking at books. He was ecstatic. "I found it. I found it!" he screamed. I looked at the book, and it was an old beat-up brown leather book, and he insisted on checking it out. He kept jumping up and down in the car with excitement. He was so anxious to get home and read it or look at it or something. When we finally got home, he quickly threw off his boots and coat, ran for the couch, and looked through the pages. I sat beside him to see what he was looking for. Then he stopped on a page in the middle of the book. There was a picture of three older men standing in a row with clothing from about the 18th century. Danny pointed to the one in the middle and excitedly screamed, "That's me; I was Rodin."

Now Danny could read most words at four, so I don't know if he read the name Rodin or if he thought he was that man. Of course, he didn't know the word reincarnation, but that's what I thought he meant. Evidently, he had a memory from another life. Rodin was a French sculptor. He carved *The Thinker* and some other famous sculptures. He was born in 1840 and died in 1917 in France when he was about seventy-seven years old. After Danny found that picture in the library book, he let go of his carving. He seems so relieved. When I tried to talk to him about Rodin, he kept insisting that is who he used to be. He would get very emotional about it, so I let it go.

Mind Reading

I was always cautious about what I was thinking around him because he sometimes could read my mind. One of the first examples of this was when he was about nine. It was about 11 p.m., and I was watching TV cuddled up on the couch when a program about bugs came on. Danny just loved bugs. I started thinking, "Oh, Dan would just love this program," but it was a school night, and I knew I shouldn't wake him up. The program got more and more interesting, and I remember thinking, "Oh, I wish Dan was here to see this, but I will have to tell him about this bug information in the morning. Oh, how I wished he could see this—it won't be the same as me repeating it to him in the morning." Suddenly, out of a deep sleep, he walked into the living room, rubbed his eyes, and said, "What do you want, Ma? What's up?" I was shocked. I had not said a word. All I had been doing was thinking. That was just one example of sometimes how he could pick up on what I was thinking. I never talked to him about my premonition. I kept that to myself, of course. But as he got older and the day got closer, I could not stop thinking about it. I just had to be careful that he was not around me when I thought about it.

Here's a little story about how Dan could read my mind. The kids were in their bedrooms getting ready for school, and I was in the kitchen trying to figure out what to fix everyone for breakfast. I thought, *Maybe eggs and bacon*, then I thought, *No, maybe pancakes*, then I thought, *Well eggs would have more nutrients than pancakes*. I was going back and forth in my mind, and I had just decided on eggs when Dan walked into the kitchen. He said, "Ma I don't mean to be fussy this morning, but I don't want those eggs that you were thinking about, I feel like pancakes this morning!"

I said, "Dan, how did you know that I was going to make eggs?"

Dan said, "I heard you."

"No, I never said anything to you. You were in your bedroom and I was in the kitchen. Did someone whisper in your ear or something?"

Dan said, "No, I just know it."

"How did you know it?"

"I knew it in my head. I just knew it in my head!" I didn't ask any more questions, but to make a long story short, we had pancakes for breakfast that morning!

Danny the Tease

Oh, how Dan would love to tease someone. He got such a kick out of that. Danny had exceptionally big hands, as I have said before. He would make them look like big claws which then would look like a big spider and then he would creep with his fingers toward you. It really looked like a big spider coming at you—creep, creep, creep—we would yell and scream. He loved to do it when we were sitting on the couch watching TV and not noticing where his claw hand was. The next thing we would know was the spider's fingers would be on our arms heading for our necks like it was going to bite us. He would then grab us and try to hug and kiss us. We liked the hugs and kisses but not the creepy crawly spider. We would laugh and scream and try to get away and run. He loved playing that game and so did we. So today when I see a spider, I just get a big smile on my face and I think of such silly good times we had when he played like he was a spider.

Danny the Chef

I grew up in the '40s in the '50s where there were women's jobs around the house and men's jobs around the house like the TV program *Leave it to Beaver*, but our household was different. It was not like that.

Our dad had died and our mom was a nurse working full time at the hospital. So, all of us kids had to do any job that had to be done regardless if it was a boy job or a girl job. Sometimes the boys would do the dishes and we girls would go out and mow the grass or shovel the snow. So that's the way I raised my kids to teach them to do anything. One evening I asked Danny to make dinner and Jackie and I would go out and shovel the driveway. We were going to have meatloaf and baked potatoes that night. I set up everything and told him how to do it. The last thing I told him about was how to do the baked potatoes. I told him to just poke a fork in each one so that they wouldn't burst in the oven. Jackie and I went out to shovel. The aroma of the dinner smelled so good after we got in from shoveling. Dan had set the table perfectly, he even had name tags on the plates where we were supposed to sit, lights were turned down dim, and soft music was playing. What a guy!

I happened to notice when we walked in that there was a whole bunch of silver shiny stuff shining through the glass in the front of the oven. But I didn't say anything to him. We sat down to eat and he proudly placed the meatloaf on a platter in front of us and then he proudly placed all the potatoes on a platter in the middle of the table with a fork sticking out of each potato. He had done exactly what I had told him to do: poke a fork in each potato, how cute is that. What a darling. He was about 10 I had neglected to tell him to pull the fork out of the potatoes before putting them in the oven. He was really good at following instructions.

Mr. Everything

Dan could fix anything. It seemed that he just naturally knew how. He fixed my broken iron, the doorbell, and a toilet. The interesting thing about this is that he knew how to do it at such a young age, like about six. How did he know how to do this? He could read at age four. He could do math problems at age five and had never been taught. He won his elementary school chess contest at the age of eight and had only been given one lesson. He could ski, having had only one lesson. He had skied his whole life, and he was only four when he was taught. He won his Boy Scout Pinewood Derby contest at age nine—with no help. He could carve—he remembered being Rodin. The scout leader said he had never seen a design like that before. It was very unusual. He was so funny. What a sense of humor he had. He was always happy and positive and an incredible friend to everyone. He was his sister Jackie's little brother and his little brother Chris's big brother. Dan was beautiful inside and out.

Danny the Helper

Danny always made projects seem easy whatever it was, it seemed like he had done it before no matter what kind of skill sets it took, nothing was ever a big production for him.

Dan was "Mr. Go To" when anyone in the neighborhood needed help with a project. He helped build patios, finish basements, and landscape yards. How he knew how to do all these things at such a young age, without any prior experience, I do not know. He seemed to have a basic understanding of all the projects he helped with.

I did not know this about him until after he passed, that in the winter after school, he would go to shovel all the neighbors' driveways, especially the neighbors that had husbands that were traveling. I just thought he was out playing with the neighbor kids. After Dan's funeral, the neighbor ladies all came up and told me how he had helped them so much but he never said a word to me.

Mr. Humble!

Mr. Zoo Man

Danny saw beauty in everything, big things little things, and simple things. In the summers he worked at the Minnesota Zoo. He absolutely loved it there. He always had a big smile for everyone and loved answering their questions and chatting with them. He especially got joy out of the little ones. Oh my, God, did he love the little ones. They just tickled the cockles of his heart! One afternoon I got a call from him at work. He had to tell me what he had just seen. It was a whole bunch of kindergartners all tied together in a line all dressed alike in red hats so they wouldn't get lost or loose. He got such a chuckle out of that. "Oh, Ma I wish you could've seen them. Ma, they were all soo cute." Can you just imagine a kid calling his mother from the zoo telling her what he had just seen and how darling it was? That's how darling he was. Danny was pure gold!

Dan the Piano Man

We called the piano "the neighborhood piano." I don't know who it started with but when one of the neighbors was through with a piano, they would pass it on to the next neighbor that wanted it. So, it went on and on. Now it was our turn to get the piano and all the kids pushed it down the street up our driveway into our laundry room. It fit just perfectly. I was in the kitchen making dinner and all the kids including Jackie and Chris and the neighbor kids were in the laundry room, when I heard someone playing the piano. It wasn't like Mozart or anything like that, it was just "Twinkle Twinkle Little Star" and "Three Blind Mice." So, I walked in to see who was playing the piano and it was Danny sitting at the piano. All the kids were clapping and laughing and Dan was going on and on like he had played it before. He had never had a lesson. Figure that one out! I asked him how he knew how to play the piano and he said," I don't know-I just knew."

CHAPTER FIVE

SIGNS FROM DAN

When loss happens, you may feel as if a part of you no longer functions. For me, I felt like I had been in a horrendous accident and I couldn't function as before and I couldn't even think straight. Some people might describe the feeling as a form of paralysis. I felt that I was still alive but that I had lost my arms and legs and I was immobilized by the horror of losing our child! Now, I had to learn how to move and navigate without my limbs. This is unbelievably painful and it takes much time to recover. It is kind of like being in grief rehab. Some days you may feel like dying, and some days you just want to sleep and rest as you do not have the stamina to continue. You don't know who you are, as you're not the same person without them. But after a while, little by little, you learn to move without your limbs and your brain starts working kind of like coming out of shock.

Although my story and feelings may be different than yours, we all go through grief rehab. You might be in rehab for the rest of your life and it isn't easy but somehow there is hope! While you are on your journey keep your heart open for signs and messages from your loved one. The messages I have received from my son are one of the many things that help me move on through my grief rehab and to know in my heart that he is OK. I just wanted to be told again and again by his messages and signs from him that he was OK and that he was close.

The signs that you receive are from your loved one acting as a physical therapist helping you move forward. Those that have passed on in your life still love you very much and are always with you cheering you on. They will give you a message or a sign for just what you needed that moment, so listen and watch. When I noticed mine, I know that Dan is telling me he is okay. Keep hope and faith in your heart and in your own way, and in your own time, you will make it!

These are just a few of the many wonderful and beautiful messages that we have received from our beloved Danny. Pick one story that you like best the one that resonates with your heart, and maybe, just maybe, you will get a message that will blow your socks off too! The message that you will receive will give you some peace and solace by letting you know that your loved one is close and they are OK!

Take A Walk

About two weeks after Dan's funeral, I was awakened one morning by someone whispering in my ear, "TAKE. A. WALK!" At first, I thought I was dreaming, but then the voice came again—only a little louder, "TAKE. A. WALK!" I opened my eyes and rolled over to see who was in my bedroom whispering that to me. But there was no one there. I rubbed my puffy swollen eyes from crying all night and looked around again, but no one was there. I lay back down—maybe I was dreaming, this was so strange, but the voice was so clear. By now I was wide awake. I quickly got up and looked out the bedroom door and down the hall to see if anyone was there. But no one! I got dressed and went to the kitchen where Jack was making coffee, I told him that I heard someone whisper in my ear twice to take a walk, I couldn't believe this was real. But I put on my tennis shoes anyway and told Jack that I would be back but that I didn't know where I was supposed to walk. I knew that I would cry, so I grabbed a terry cloth towel and went out the door. As I was leaving, I thought that I should take a bigger towel, as I had told everyone that there were more than 10,000 lakes in Minnesota with me crying, any way out the door I went. I didn't have a clue where to go, so I just started walking up the hill beside our house. When I got to the top of the hill, I didn't know which way to go, left or right. Then I noticed some neighborhood walkers on the left so I turned to the right. I didn't feel like talking to the neighbors right then. The turn to the right was perfect as there were no people and no houses and just an empty field beside the sidewalk. After walking for about 1/4 of a mile, through my tears, something caught my eye. It was a big yellow balloon blowing in the wind with its string caught on some weeds next to the sidewalk. It was like the balloon was waving at me and saying "hello." Oh my God! Yellow was Dan's favorite color! How could I miss it? No way! So, I ran over to the balloon and started untangling the string from the weeds when I spotted something stuck to the bottom of the string. It was a Wheatie penny. I was in shock; I couldn't believe my eyes. I carefully untangled the penny from the string. Danny and grandma Viv had collected Wheaties since he was a little boy. He had a huge collection. I looked at the date and it was the date that Dan and grandma Viv had always been looking for. I took the balloon and penny home. The message was both heart-breaking and heartwarming, for I felt he was trying to tell me that he was OK. That was very comforting—at least that was the way I chose to see it. I needed that message. It for sure blew my socks off! It was his second message since the wake and he was starting to tell us with many messages in the future that he was OK on the other side!!

When I got home, of course I told Jack about it. I didn't know if I should tell Jackie and Chris. Would they think I had made the story up or would they think that I was just totally nuts? If they did believe it, would they think it was just a coincidence, or would it make them sad and cry? I didn't know what to do, so I just kept it to my-self.

Lois

It was October 1, 1985, five months after Dan had passed and I was having a party at our house for Chris's baseball team. It was the end of the baseball season and we had invited his team members over to our house for a party. I was torn, as my dear friend Lois was in the hospital dying and I had gone over to the hospital to say goodbye to her but I had to get back to the house for the party. A few months before, Lois and I had made a pact that she would check on Dan when she passed, wherever she was, and let me know that he was OK and I would check on her son who was still in high school. Her husband, son, a friend, and I were all standing by her bedside and she was trying to talk but her speech was not legible. Nobody was understanding what she was saying, except me. I knew exactly what she was saying. She was saying "Phyllis, I will check on Danny and let you know!" I figured that her family would probably want to be alone with her when she passed, so I kissed Lois goodbye and told her I loved her and gave her family hugs and left. When I arrived home, the party was in full swing. Chris was holding down the fort and I had made the food the day before just in case I was late for the party. It was a gorgeous beautiful evening and we had both the front doors wide open. The boys were coming and going and having a lot of fun. I could see that all was going well and the boys probably didn't want me hanging around, so I decided to go back to my bedroom and read my new *People* magazine. My bedroom is right down the hall from the front door, and around the corner, I could hear all the boys laughing, talking, and carrying on. Shortly after I got to my room, I heard the doorbell ring. I heard a woman's voice ask one of the boys where I was and I heard him tell her that I was in my bedroom. I looked up from my magazine and as hard as it is to believe—there stood Lois—she just looked absolutely beautiful and she had a gorgeous long flowing kind of silvery-looking dress on. Her hair was so pretty and she was just glowing. I don't know why but I just said to her, "Lois, what are you doing here?"

She said "I've come to tell you Danny is OK," and with that, she turned and went out the bedroom door. I leaped up and ran around to the bottom of the bed toward the door. When I got there, she wasn't there. I ran to the foyer. She wasn't there. I looked outside she wasn't there. Where did she go? This made no sense. She was nowhere in sight. I turned around and asked the boy who had let her in and had told her that I was in my room if he had seen her leave. He said no he had just let her in. All I could think of to do was to go get a picture of Lois that I had recently taken and show the boy a picture of her and I asked him if that was the lady that he had let in. And he said, "Yep that's her, that's the lady." This was unknown territory for me, nothing like this had ever happened to me before. I learned later that the time she had appeared to me was at the exact time that she had passed. A few days later when I was going to her wake, I picked up my sister to go with me. It was dark at about 7 p.m. and real foggy. We decided to take a shortcut to the funeral home and go by the Burnsville Hospital so we wouldn't have to go out on a busy road with the fog being so dense. I was driving slow in front of the hospital when all of a sudden, a dirty white Red Cross truck with a big red cross on the side pulled out right in front of us. If I would have been going any faster, we would've hit it. Just as we were saying that to each other, both of us became aware at the same time that there was writing on the back of the dirty Red Cross truck. On the truck's dirty back, something was written in the dirt. It said—He's OK. Fran and I couldn't believe it. Thank God Fran was with me to witness this. We both were in shock!

Acre by Acre

A couple of months after Dan had passed, I took my mother to a local hospital for a colonoscopy. When we got there, the lobby was packed. There must've been twenty-five people waiting for different procedures. We eyeballed the room for a place to sit. Finally, a lovely lady noticed that we were looking for a place, and she moved one seat over so we could sit together. We settled in and waited for a long wait as mom likes to be early. She always said, "If you're on time, you're late," so true to form, we were there early for her appointment.

As we chatted and read the newspaper, I noticed an older man from across the room staring at us. He looked to be around eighty years old. He was wearing baggy old bib overalls and had a farmer tan where his cap had covered his head but not his forehead and had left a distinct tan line. I nudged mom and said, "Don't look now but is that man over there on the other side of the room staring at me or you?" She peeked from behind her newspaper and quietly said, "He is staring at you." Good heavens, with all the people in that room, why was he looking at me? As the time went on, maybe twenty or thirty minutes, he kept looking at me. I was becoming very uncomfortable. I kept trying to hide behind my newspaper. Finally, mom was called in for her appointment, which left an empty chair next to me. Sure enough, I knew it. The older man came and sat down beside me. He just started talking to me, and I couldn't ignore him. I did not want to be rude, so I put my newspaper down and started listening.

I was feeling down and depressed over Danny, and I didn't want to talk to anyone. I just wanted to say, "Leave me alone, leave me alone, " but he kept talking. He said, "You know I'm a farmer from outside town, and I have farmed here for over sixty years. My family insists that I sell my beloved farm and move into town. I would be confronted with making a new life for myself without my farm. How do I become someone else without it? I love my farm. I will miss my farm. I can't live without my farm." He started to cry, and I could feel his grief. I tried to comfort him, but he said there would be a big hole in his heart if his family made him do this. He couldn't let go of his farm.

I pulled a Kleenex out of my purse and gave him one and one for me. We must've looked like a couple of wackos sitting in the lobby crying, one soul helping another soul. That was precisely what was happening. One soul assisting another soul. How strange. Then he said something that stopped my heart. He said, "but I will be OK." There were those words again. He said, "Do you know what I'm going to do?" I said, "No, how are you going to get through this?" He said, "Well, depending on how long I live, I am going to sell my farm acre by acre. and that will give me time to figure out the new me without my farm." I felt a sudden tingle. I took this to mean that Dan was there and telling me to listen to this older man. Then they called his name, and he got up very slowly and went in for his appointment. I never saw him again. What an analogy. Learning how to live with a major loss.

This unexpected lesson was delivered straight from Dan through an older man. What a message. This seemed too much of a message to be just a coincidence. This message blew my socks off.

Ryan

It was Danny's first birthday since he passed. He would have been 23. Jackie had invited us out for dinner. Jack and I went out to her house in two cars because I would be through working at two, and he would not get off work until five. If I came out early, I thought I could play with darling little Ryan and take him out on the driveway and play because it was such a beautiful day. So while

Jackie was fixing dinner, Ryan and I went out to play on the driveway. The garage door was open, and inside the garage, there was a little table set up with paper and pencils, coloring books, and sidewalk chalk. He was such a happy little camper. He rode his little trike up and down the driveway. Then, when he got bored, he would go to his little table and color and draw. I enjoyed the fall sun sitting in a lawn chair alongside the driveway, watching him play.

I could see he was getting bored with his trike, so he rode it into the garage and sat down at his little table; he was busy drawing when suddenly he got up and came over to me with a bit of piece of paper in his hand and handed it to me. This is what it said. First, Dan, then Danny, and a birthday cake drawing with candles on it. He asked me, "Grandma, what did I write?" I was stunned. He was 2 ½ and didn't know how to write, and he did not know it was Danny's birthday—.As I was looking at his little note, he ran over and got his sidewalk chalk and started to write something on the driveway. He wrote with Dan's favorite color, yellow. I couldn't believe my eyes. My heart was pounding, and I started to cry. At that moment, Jack pulled up and got out of his car to see what Ryan was writing on the driveway.

Jack was blown away, too. He couldn't believe what he was seeing. It said the same thing. Dan. But then, in cursive Danny. This is no coincidence. I didn't want to upset Jackie before dinner, so after dinner, while Jack and Ryan's dad played with Ryan, I took her outside and showed her the writing on the driveway and the little note. She couldn't believe it. She asked if I had written it. I said no. Jack had seen him writing on the driveway too. Then I showed her the note. We both started crying. She said she did not tell Ryan it was Danny's birthday as she didn't want to upset him, besides, he did not even know Danny. How did he know it was Dan's birthday, and how did he know how to write Dan's name, especially in cursive? I said, "I don't know how he could know this as I had never said anything about Dan's birthday to him." We both stood there in disbelief. Danny had come to us through Ryan. Dan let us know that "he was OK" and sent a powerful and unbelievable message that he was with us. And most likely that we should be OK too. This blew my socks off.

I have read that when a soul is trying to reach the mind of a grieving parent, they sometimes use children as conduits for their messages. I guess children are more receptive to spirits because they have not been conditioned to block a spirit. Many times, the spirit is the departed member of the family. Well, we sure listened to our Dan reaching us through Ryan.

Ryan's handwritten note

Picture Frame

It was Danny's 24th birthday and, like usual, I would ask him to send a message that would blow my socks off every year. I had waited all day and received nothing. Like a couple of times before, it was when a message finally would come at the end of the day. I still had hope for a message even as it was getting late. I was at my massage spa at the Holiday Inn hotel, cleaning up at the end of the day. As I walked through the hotel lobby to leave, I noticed a client who got her haircut at the beauty shop where I have another massage spa. She was sitting on a chair by the front door. On her lap was a beautifully wrapped little box. As I went up to her to say hi, she said, "Hi Phyllis, I've been waiting for you. I heard from Katie (the beauty shop owner) that you had lost your son. I brought you something." She handed me the box, and I sat down beside her and thought, *Oh, how nice of her.* She had come over to the hotel and waited for me, not knowing when I would be done working. I asked her if I could open the gift now, and she said, "Of course." So, I carefully opened it. Inside was a beautiful gold picture frame. What a shock. I had been looking for months for just the right picture frame to put Danny's picture in and couldn't find one that I liked. I had looked all over for the right frame but to no avail. And here it was, just perfect and even the correct size. How could she show up on Dan's birthday with just the right picture frame I had been looking for? Danny was again telling me that he was OK. That blew my socks off.

St. Cloud Guy

It was Danny's 25th birthday, and that morning I had asked for another message from him. I was exhausted. I was working at my massage business and had given about seven or eight full-body deep massages that day. It was about 7:30 p.m., and I just wanted to go home, shower, and collapse into bed. I was in the middle of cleaning up my massage room and gathering up the dirty laundry when the receptionist from the shop came running into my room. She asked if I would give one more massage to a man in the lobby who had come to the Burnsville area from Saint Cloud to help his son build a deck. He had worked all day, and his back was in great distress. I peeked through the crack in the door, and I could see him holding his back. I hardly had any energy or strength left, and I was so tired, but how could I possibly tell him no. I told her to tell him yes, I would give him a massage. I got the room ready for one more massage. He was a big man, and he looked like he had a back the size of Texas. I took off my coat and set the dirty laundry down, and told the receptionist to tell him to come in. He introduced himself and said he was so grateful and kept thanking me and thanking me. Somehow, I got renewed strength to give one more massage. Some people seem to like to talk during massages, and he was one of them. I just listened while he told me all about himself. He said he was from the Saint Cloud area and had been employed investigating something called stray voltage that was electricity running through the ground making farm animals and people sick. He also owned a small grocery store in Saint Joseph where all the boys from Saint John's came in to purchase items. He said he had met so many wonderful boys from Saint John's, but there was one boy that was very special. With that, my ears perked up. Until then, I had been half asleep and was only half-listening. It was 8:00 p.m., and I had not gotten a message from Dan, yet I remember thinking, here it is. Suddenly, he starts talking about this wonderful boy from Saint John's that would come into his store and how special this boy was. He had met hundreds of boys throughout the years, but this boy was extraordinary. He told me that the boy was about six feet two inches tall, handsome as hell, and super intelligent. But he said above all. The boy was such a loving kid. I almost fainted. I know he was talking about Danny. He told me he had heard the boy had died. After he had finished helping his son build the deck, he planned to look up the boy's mother. The boy had told him that he lived in Burnsville. Thank God I was just finished with the massage when he started to cry. I was crying too, but he couldn't see me. Afterward, I told him that there would be no charge. I asked was the boy named Danny. He squinted his eyes at me and asked, "Are you, his mother? "I said yes. Oh my God. We both hugged and cried. He said he had a big place in his heart for Danny as big tears rolled down his face. He said," I just loved that kid."

That message blew my socks off. Thanks, Dan.

The Birds

I got up to make Dan's favorite cookie. It was his birthday and I always made chocolate chip cookies for the occasion. Mary, my cleaning lady, had just walked in, and I was hurrying so that when she got to the kitchen to clean, I would be done baking. She always started cleaning in the back of the house by the bedrooms. Suddenly, she started yelling, "Phyllis, Phyllis, come here quick!" I put down my mixer and ran toward the bedroom she was cleaning. She was in Danny's room and was staring at the window. "Look," she said, "that red bird won't stop pecking at the window. I tried to scare it away, but it wouldn't go." We just stood there staring at the bird that was trying to get our attention. After about a minute, it stopped, looked at us, and flew away. I thought, *Oh, that was a message from Dan.* It was a sweet message for the bird to peck on his bedroom window. That was not the blow my socks off kind of message, but I was thankful for the message. Then I got a surprise. Mary never said anything, but she was freaked out because she was in Danny's bedroom. I went back to the kitchen to finish my cookies when I heard some pecking on our dining room window. I turned around, and the little red bird was pecking at the dining room window. I went into the dining room and started staring at it, and after about a minute, it flew away. The next minute it was at the kitchen window pecking. So, I scurried back to the kitchen. I looked out the kitchen window and saw some action by Dan's tree. It was the tree he had planted when he was about eleven years old. Hundreds of brown birds were sitting on his tree. I couldn't believe what I was seeing. I had never seen so many birds in one place. I felt like I was in the Alfred Hitchcock movie *The Birds*." There, sitting in the middle of the bunch of birds, proud as punch, was the little red bird that we had seen pecking at our windows. Of course, I thought, that must be Dan, and he had invited all his friends to his birthday party. I brought the cookies out for the party and laid them on the grass under the tree. They were all gone about an hour later, and so were the birds. The party was over.

Now that blew my socks off.

Heart

One day, I was sitting on Danny's bedroom floor, wondering how I could turn his room into Jack's office. Not only physically but emotionally. But it was time. It had been a couple of years since Danny had died, and I know he would have wanted us to move on. So, I started scraping the wallpaper off the bedroom walls that he had helped me put on. It seemed like I was scraping him away, but then I thought, don't think that way. Think with every scrape that you're letting his soul go and fly wherever he wants. So, with every scrape, that's what I thought. I had taken down the blinds from the bedroom windows a few weeks before and ordered some different ones from Sears. Jack came in to help me, and just then, the phone rang, and it was Sears. They told me that my order was in. I desperately wanted to get them to see if they would fit the windows and if they looked like what I had imagined. But there was a big snowstorm going on.

The shopping center where Sears was located wasn't too far from our house, and I knew I could make it. But Jack kept saying, "Don't go. There's no rush—wait till tomorrow." But something just kept telling me to go. I looked outside, trying to see what was going on, and the snowstorm was terrible. My voice of reason said no, don't go. It can wait. But something kept saying go. The voice of reason did not win out. I bundled up, checked the car for gas, and off I went. I was floored when I finally got to Sears and the merchandise pick-up department. There was a long line of maybe fifteen people waiting to pick up their orders. You would have thought it was a beautiful summer day outside instead of a winter snowstorm. I stood in line waiting my turn when suddenly an announcement came over the loudspeaker.

The announcement said that there would be a drawing for a piece of jewelry in the Sears jewelry department in about 45 minutes—so come over and register. My inner voice said, "You're almost to the merchandise pickup counter so stay in line." But the other voice said, "Go. That's why you're supposed to be here." I *knew* if I registered for the drawing, I would win. I just *knew* it. That is why I was supposed to be here. The man behind me said, "Hey lady, are you going to move or stand here all day." I left the line and ran to the jewelry department. I registered for the jewelry drawing and ran back to the merchandise pick-up line. Just as I was almost to the head of the line again, there was an announcement over the loudspeaker: "Would Phyllis Schwartz please come to the jewelry department." I left the line again and ran back to the jewelry department, where they told me that I had won the jewelry prize. They presented me with a beautiful diamond heart on a sterling silver chain—what a message. I held the diamond heart close to my heart and ran back to the end of the merchandise pick-up line to pick up my window blinds. When I got home with my blinds, I didn't even care what they looked like. I just sat and held the diamond heart close to my heart and kept looking at it all day. I was supposed to venture out in that storm. Thanks for the message, Dan—I love my diamond heart. What a gift.

Delivery Man

At 7:00 a.m. on another of Dan's birthdays, I asked him again to knock my socks off with a message. We were almost out of massage oil at my massage center, and if the delivery didn't come by 3:00 p.m., we could not give any more massages that day. I was sitting at the front desk facing the window that looked out onto the parking lot. I was watching for the oil delivery and also making appointments. It had been almost eight hours since I had asked for a message, and I had not received anything, and I was starting to feel anxious. Just about that time, I saw a big delivery truck pull up in front of the shopping center, and I assumed that it must be our massage oil being delivered. I saw a man get out of the delivery truck carrying a big box and heading for the front door of our shop. I thought to myself, *Is this my message that the oil is coming in on time?* Not that I wasn't grateful, but I thought this was not like the clever and unique messages that Danny usually sent. Like, knock my socks off type messages. The phone rang just as the man was coming in the door with the massage oil. It was a client requesting a massage appointment. Just as I finished making the appointment, I looked up and saw a big pair of hands coming down over the top of the desk, palms up. I freaked. Those were Dan's big hands. They looked exactly like Dan's hands. I looked up, and the delivery man said, "I've come to pray for you—and your family. I feel you have lost a child" and he reached out and took both of my hands and said a prayer. I was in shock. Before I could say anything, he turned around and left. I had never seen him before, and I've never seen him since. This was wonderful because just as the man came in carrying in the oil, a massage therapist came in from the back room, and she heard and saw the whole thing. She said, "What was that all about?"

Facebook Sign

Danny likes to involve other people in his messages.

It wasn't Dan's birthday, but I wanted to hear from him. In the early morning or the early evening, the veil to the universe is very thin, so that's an excellent time to meditate or ask for something. I don't know if that is true or not, but that is usually when I meditate and talk to whoever wants to listen. I am also very good at what Deepak Chopra calls slipping into the gap (meaning a blank non-thinking place where you let the universe take care of the details) I taught myself how to do that while giving massages, focusing on nothing, just slipping between the synapse in your brain. It also made the time go fast because I was in a dark room hour after hour, giving massages. I had time to practice and practice the process to get through my massages, so just like a lot of mornings, I meditated, and then I thought I would ask Dan if he would send me a message or a sign or something. I got up, dressed, and went to the kitchen for breakfast. As I was enjoying my breakfast, I suddenly got an urge to check my Facebook. The very first thing that popped up was this:

"As I sit in heaven and watch you every day, I try to let you know with signs I never went away. I hear you when you're laughing and watch you while you sleep. I even placed my arms around you to calm you as you weep. I see you wish the day away, begging to have me home, so I try to send you signs so you know you're not alone. Don't feel guilty that you have the life that was denied to me; heaven is truly beautiful; just you wait and see. So, live your life, laugh again, enjoy yourself, be free. Then I know with every breath you take you'll be taking one for me."

Omg.

How could I get a reply so fast? Dan must be on Facebook too. Thank you, Dan. That message was beyond perfect!

Logging Truck

Sometimes I just get help without even asking for it. I always seemed to know that good vibes and energy were around me. It was like my guardian angel or Danny, or somebody was always protecting me. One day I was going out to see my mom and sister, who lived in Prior Lake. There is a big hairpin turn right before you get to their house. The hairpin curve goes up quickly and makes a sharp curve down quickly. I could see a huge logging truck coming up on the other side of the curve through the woods. I remember thinking, that's strange. I've never seen a logging truck here before. Then in the next second, a voice in my head or ear, I don't know, said, "Get off the road—get off the road." So, in that second, I turned right off the road into a driveway in front of a house, and as I pulled in, I heard a crash. I looked behind me in the rearview mirror, and just where I would've been, the logging truck had tipped over with all its logs. I would have been crushed to death— I chose to believe that Dan was communicating with me again and protecting me. Thank you, Dan, for saving my life.

A Client Mr. Hill

An older man came to my massage center for a massage. He was dying of brain cancer, and he was so sick. He had already had two rounds of chemo, and his family wanted him to have another one, but he said no. Enough is enough. His doctor had suggested a massage for him just for some relaxation. He had never had a massage before, and he was so scared. But we chatted for a while before the massage, and I got him to loosen up and even laugh. During the massage, he wanted to talk about what had happened to him and what he was going through. The poor thing. Then he started talking about his life and hobbies, sports, and interests. I just listened. One of his interests was Apple Valley football, as he lived in Apple Valley. He had made friends with one of the boys on the team. The boy would come early to practice and sit with him on the bleachers, and the kid would give him encouragement about his brain cancer. They became very close friends. He never had a son, and if he had had a son, he would have wanted one just like this boy. Sometimes the boy would bring snacks such as cookies that his mom had made then the boy would help him back to his car. Anyway, the boy graduated from high school, and they continued to talk on the phone. He said the kid went to St. John's and that's when my ears picked up. After about three and a half years, he never heard from the boy again. The boy always kept in touch, and that was not like him. He just stopped communicating. He didn't write and didn't call— Again, that wasn't like the boy to just drop me, because he knew I was dying.

After the massage, just like the other client I had, I asked him if the boy's name was Dan. He gulped and said yes. I had to tell him that Danny had died and that I was Dan's mother. He just crumbled to the floor. I picked him up and got him to a chair. He was just sobbing. He said, "I knew. something was wrong—big time wrong. I just loved him. I have never met anybody like him since." After that, I never saw the man again. But about two months later, I saw his obituary in the local paper. At this point, I think that there are no such things as coincidences. Danny's ability to communicate was unbelievable. He was alive someplace, and he was really OK. Thanks again. It made me feel good to see what a lasting impression Dan has made on people.

Dan the Rock Hound

Of course, I had heard many stories of people getting signs and messages after a loved one had passed, but some of those stories were too far-fetched and hard to believe. Others I thought might be wishful thinking, others I thought just might just plain be lies. But now I was in the middle of it myself. I was one of them! How do you explain these things to people and not have them look at you like "Oh yeah?" My thinking started to change when I begin receiving more and more messages from Dan that all left me in disbelief. I hope that by reading my book and some of my stories you'll get some reassurance and comfort that your loved ones are OK—just as I did.

It was my birthday on February 5th and we didn't have much planned. Maybe we would go to see our grandchildren that night. As I got up, I asked Dan to send me a message today that would knock my socks off. I didn't really expect any messages but I just thought I'd ask anyway. I went on with my morning chores. I showered, made the bed, threw some towels in the washer, picked up the kitchen, and made a grocery list. As I was putting the towels from the washer into the dryer, the phone rang. I quickly ran from the laundry room to the kitchen to answer it. It was a girlfriend calling. As we were chatting, she said, "Phyllis what is that clunking sound in the background?" I hadn't really heard it as I was listening to her. So, I stopped and listened and sure enough, there was a little clunking sound coming from the laundry room. I told my friend the sound might be coming from the dryer and I would check on it and call her back. As I went into the laundry room, yes indeed, the noise was coming from the dryer. I opened the dryer and started to pull the towels out and there at the bottom of the tub was something hard and round. I reached in and pulled it out. Holy moly it was a rose quartz gemstone! My favorite of all gemstones! Rose quartz is calming to a person holding it. It increases the power of telepathic transmissions and increases psychic awareness. I had carried one in my pocket for years. I learned about gemstones when I was young from my aunt and uncle that lived in Arizona. So, when we realized Dan was so enthralled with rocks and stones, we bought him a rock tumbler to polish them. He absolutely loved it. The tumbler ran 24 seven and the stones turned out just beautiful. But as I said, my favorite was that rose quartz, and Dan knew it and he always tried to find them for me. How could a rose quartz stone end up in my dryer? We had put all his collection in a container in the closet several years ago. But I had asked him for a sign and it was my birthday but this was unbelievable. No one was in the house except me and Jack, but my friend had heard the clunking in the dryer too! How do you explain this message to someone? Who was going to believe it? This sign was so Danny! Thanks again.

Jake

Now Danny's younger brother Chris was through college, married, and he and his wife Lori were expecting their first child. Jake came two weeks early on November 4, 1997, at 11:00 a.m. He weighed 9 lb. 9 oz. and we were all so excited. Chris called me and Lori's mother Judy and told us that Lori was in labor at the hospital. So Judy and I jumped in the car and headed for the Southdale hospital. But Jake got stuck in the birth canal, so before they were going to do a C-section Lori asked me if I would do some foot reflexology on her. Miraculously, Jake flipped, and he got to have a normal birth. We each got to hold him and take pictures. Chris was holding him when the phone rang. Lori reached over and picked it up. She said hello. Dead silence on the other end—then Lori asked, "Who is this?" The person on the other end said, "This is Dan" and hung up. Lori had a strange look on her face. I was standing at the foot of the bed with Judy and asked her who it was. Lori said it was Dan. I said, "I believe it." Lori had never met Dan, as she started dating Chris after Dan had passed. She thought he was calling her just to connect with her to say hi. They named the baby Jake Daniel—after Danny! Now our darling Jake grew up and it was time for him to graduate. We were all happy for him but sad at the same time—because every time one of our grandchildren got to graduate, we always thought in the back of our mind that our Danny had never got to walk up to receive his diploma. Now it was time for Jake to walk up on stage and get his diploma and to our astonishment, the superintendent of schools made a mistake and called him Daniel—Jake—Schwartz. Danny got to walk!

Swan Dog

October 11, 2017. As usual, I asked for a message from Dan. I never knew what to expect, but his messages often come through people. But like I had asked him before, "Please don't make it look just like a coincidence, or I won't notice it. The sign has to knock my socks off." I waited all day—nothing. Then, about six at night, the phone rang. Jack answered it. Oh my God—it was Swan Dog. — Swan Dog was Danny's very best friend in the whole world. They had been friends for years and years. They were inseparable. They both loved the same things. Tinkering, building stuff, working at a pizza place, and football. Dan was six feet two—Swan Dog was six feet five. Both were tall and thin. We had not heard from him or seen him since the day of the funeral 32 years ago. He had gone to college, become an engineer, married, had a family, and had just dropped out of sight. I think it was just too painful for him to see us. Anyway, on the night of Danny's birthday, he called. We chatted and got caught up. I can't imagine how hard that must've been for him to make that call, but at the end of the conversation, he said that he had wanted to call us for years, but tonight, Danny just kept telling him to contact us, and he always did what Dan wanted him to do— Dan was the boss. Then we asked him if he knew that it was Dan's birthday today—-he said he did not. Wow, that knocked my socks off. Thanks, Dan. I know you're telling us that you're OK and that we should be OK, and that Swan Dog was finally OK too.

Feathers

Danny loved feathers. There wasn't much of anything that he didn't love. When he was a little boy, and I would do laundry, I would always make sure that I checked all his pockets since you never knew what you would find in them. Almost anything could be in those pockets—rocks, stones, and bugs seemed to be his main collections. When I found feathers, he always knew what bird they came from, and evidently different colored feathers have different meanings and he would tell me what the feather meant. He liked the white feathers best. In the winter when it snowed, he would watch and wait to see if the snow would come down like big white feathers. When it did, he would run outside and try to catch them with his tongue. He would whirl around and around—arms stretched out like an airplane—trying to catch those big snowflake feathers. Then he would come in, his face all red, huffing and puffing, with a big smile on his face. He just loved those big snowflakes that looked like big feathers! So today when I see them, I know he's real close and I can just see him outside swirling around and swirling around, trying to catch those big flakes with his tongue.

One day this winter while it was snowing, we received a phone call from Ann, our publisher who was doing Danny's book. During our conversation, it turned to a specific story about Danny. At that exact moment, the snow outside turned into big snowflakes that looked like feathers, and when we hung up from the call the feathers immediately stopped! Maybe this was more like a coincidence, but it felt like a message—such perfect timing! A white feather means all is well, and peace and love. That's what I felt like listening to Ann's voice.

CHAPTER SIX

CONCLUSION

E ach one of us will experience grief and sorrow at some point in our life's journey, and we will each need to work through the deep emotions that accompany it. For me, receiving signs that had a special meaning to my son and me helped me to feel that our connection remained for me to move forward with my life.

I was just an ordinary, 22-year-old, new mother who was given an extraordinary glimpse of the brief future of my son's life and a graphic image of his death.

Some could look at it as a "gift"—that the veil between worlds parted briefly for me to see this vision. I knew I must cherish every moment I had with him going forward. The plans I made for my child and the dreams for their future weighed heavy on me.

You might say that my grief began on that very day and continued with dread of the date 5-22-1985 yet to come. Could I change things or was it beyond my control? Was I better off not knowing? Or was I better off knowing so that I could cherish each moment with him? Once the premonition was fulfilled, a new more devastating grief and sorrow filled me. The deeper grief of a parent losing their child now took its place.

Danny had supported me in fulfilling my dream in life to have my own massage business. Once I created "Keep in Touch" and had numerous clients over the past 40 years, I was amazed by the many stories I heard of them receiving signs from loved ones that had passed or were about to pass. It became evident that by keeping your heart open and being receptive to signs that a connection could remain.

Yes, indeed, I have had a miracle in my life. My child may not be here in person, but he is convincing me with his messages that he is still alive and OK. He wants me to be OK, too. That thought has given me peace. I know he wants me to be happy and that his spirit remains with me always.

Be gentle with yourself on your grief journey. Give yourself permission to talk and cry with your loved ones, take joy in finding an unexpected shiny penny, view a stunning rainbow that suddenly appeared just for you, a bird or a butterfly that takes a very long time keeping you company in your presence, a remembered scent that you both shared, or even through people making unusual connections to your loved one, as my son did for me so often. Keep the hope that you are still connected with your loved one and that you are communicating now on a different plane. Your bond of love remains and is not broken.

Through the numerous signs that I have received from Danny, I *know* that he is okay! And I just want to say,

"Dear Danny,

You knew I didn't have the courage to write this book, so I want to thank you for nudging and prodding me to write OUR story. Thank you for finding what I had visualized for the cover of this book that tells the story, artist Rodisley da Silva, from Brazil. Thank you for miraculously being led to our editor and our publisher, Ann Aubitz, and thank you to my friend, Pam Foster, who fostered me in this process, and last but not least thank you to Jack, who has stood by me throughout this whole process. We all did it together! Danny, I am OK! Love you always and forever, MOM."

LEGACIES AND COMPLIMENTS

Legacies:

- Dan was an organ donor and donated his eyes at the time of his passing.
- We set up a foundation at St. Johns in Dan's memory and donated the money we received from his funeral to be given to qualifying business students.
- I started my massage business and named it "Keep in Touch" in memory of Dan and later started the first massage franchise in the entire nation. The name "Keep in Touch" really meant "Keep in Touch Danny."

Compliments:

At Dan's funeral, there were hundreds of people, and hundreds of wonderful things were said about Danny. I hang on to two very special compliments from two of his college buddies.

1) "What was so wonderful about Dan was that he didn't know how wonderful he was"

2) "I loved Dan even after I got to know him"

CPSIA information can be obtained
at www.ICGtesting.com
Printed in the USA
LVHW080700300722
724782LV00016B/876

9 781952 976551